Creating Global Bonds, Grade 12

T0326171

What if you could challenge your twelfth-grade students to explore energy consumption and climate change in their own communities, and connect that information with other communities around the world? With this volume in the *STEM Road Map Curriculum Series*, you can!

Creating Global Bonds outlines a journey that will steer your students toward authentic problem solving while grounding them in integrated STEM disciplines. Like the other volumes in the series, this book is designed to meet the growing need to infuse real-world learning into K–12 classrooms.

This interdisciplinary, three-lesson module uses project- and problem-based learning to help students create an action plan to address issues of energy consumption and climate change, exploring the topic at both local and global levels. Students will gather data on energy consumption and climate change in their communities, partnering with international students to undertake problem-solving activities that examine issues that are both common and unique to each community.

To support this goal, students will do the following:

- Identify modes and trends in energy consumption in their communities and regions;

- Analyze how those patterns of energy consumption impact climate change;

- Partner with students internationally to coordinate efforts to synthesize energy consumption data and discern connections across contexts, taking the form of an international blog;

- Design and present an action plan to address issues of energy consumption and climate change, ultimately delivering a white paper and interactive web-based presentation on local and international issues of energy consumption and climate change.

The *STEM Road Map Curriculum Series* is anchored in the Next Generation Science Standards, the Common Core State Standards, and the Framework for 21st Century Learning. In-depth and flexible, *Creating Global Bonds* can be used as a whole unit or in part to meet the needs of districts, schools, and teachers who are charting a course toward an integrated STEM approach.

Carla C. Johnson is a Professor of Science Education and Office of Research and Innovation Faculty Research Fellow at North Carolina State University, North Carolina, USA.

Janet B. Walton is a Senior Research Scholar at North Carolina State's College of Education in Raleigh, North Carolina, USA.

Erin E. Peters-Burton is the Donna R. and David E. Sterling Endowed Professor in Science Education at George Mason University in Fairfax, Virginia, USA.

THE STEM ROAD MAP CURRICULUM SERIES

Series editors: Carla C. Johnson, Janet B. Walton, and Erin E. Peters-Burton

Map out a journey that will steer your students toward authentic problem solving as you ground them in integrated STEM disciplines.

Co-published by Routledge and NSTA Press, in partnership with the National Science Teaching Association, this K–12 curriculum series is anchored in the Next Generation Science Standards, the Common Core State Standards, and the Framework for 21st Century Learning. It was developed to meet the growing need to infuse real-world STEM learning into classrooms.

Each book is an in-depth module that uses project- and problem-based learning. First, your students are presented with a challenge. Then, they apply what they learn using science, social studies, English language arts, and mathematics. Engaging and flexible, each volume can be used as a whole unit or in part to meet the needs of districts, schools, and teachers who are charting a course toward an integrated STEM approach.

Modules are available from NSTA Press and Routledge, and organized under the following themes. For an update listing of the volumes in the series, please visit https://www.routledge.com/STEM-Road-Map-Curriculum-Series/book-series/SRM (for titles co-published by Routledge and NSTA Press), or www.nsta.org/book-series/stem-road-map-curriculum (for titles published by NSTA Press).

Co-published by Routledge and NSTA Press:

Optimizing the Human Experience:

- *Our Changing Environment, Grade K: STEM Road Map for Elementary School*
- *Genetically Modified Organisms, Grade 7: STEM Road Map for Middle School*
- *Rebuilding the Natural Environment, Grade 10: STEM Road Map for High School*
- *Mineral Resources, Grade 11: STEM Road Map for High School*

Cause and Effect:

- *Formation of the Earth, Grade 9: STEM Road Map for High School*

Published by NSTA Press:

Innovation and Progress:

- *Amusement Park of the Future, Grade 6: STEM Road Map for Elementary School*
- *Transportation in the Future, Grade 3: STEM Road Map for Elementary School*
- *Harnessing Solar Energy, Grade 4: STEM Road Map for Elementary School*
- *Wind Energy, Grade 5: STEM Road Map for Elementary School*
- *Construction Materials, Grade 11: STEM Road Map for High School*

The Represented World:

- *Patterns and the Plant World, Grade 1: STEM Road Map for Elementary School*

- *Investigating Environmental Changes, Grade 2: STEM Road Map for Elementary School*
- *Swing Set Makeover, Grade 3: STEM Road Map for Elementary School*
- *Rainwater Analysis, Grade 5: STEM Road Map for Elementary School*
- *Packaging Design, Grade 6: STEM Road Map for Middle School*
- *Improving Bridge Design, Grade 8: STEM Road Map for Middle School*
- *Radioactivity, Grade 11: STEM Road Map for High School*
- *Car Crashes, Grade 12: STEM Road Map for High School*

Cause and Effect:

- *Physics in Motion, Grade K: STEM Road Map for Elementary School*
- *Influence of Waves, Grade 1: STEM Road Map for Elementary School*
- *Natural Hazards, Grade 2: STEM Road Map for Elementary School*
- *Human Impacts on Our Climate, Grade 6: STEM Road Map for Middle School*
- *The Changing Earth, Grade 8: STEM Road Map for Middle School*
- *Healthy Living, Grade 10: STEM Road Map for High School*

Creating Global Bonds

Grade
12

STEM Road Map
for High School

Edited by Carla C. Johnson, Janet B. Walton,
and Erin E. Peters-Burton

Routledge
Taylor & Francis Group

NEW YORK AND LONDON

nsta Press
National Science Teaching Association

Designed cover image: © Getty Images and © Shutterstock

First published 2023
by Routledge
605 Third Avenue, New York, NY 10158

and by Routledge
4 Park Square, Milton Park, Abingdon, Oxon, OX14 4RN

Routledge is an imprint of the Taylor & Francis Group, an informa business

A co-publication with NSTA Press

© 2023 selection and editorial matter, National Science Teaching Association; individual chapters, the contributors

The right of Carla C. Johnson, Janet B. Walton, and Erin E. Peters-Burton to be identified as the authors of the editorial material, and of the authors for their individual chapters, has been asserted in accordance with sections 77 and 78 of the Copyright, Designs and Patents Act 1988.

All rights reserved. No part of this book may be reprinted or reproduced or utilised in any form or by any electronic, mechanical, or other means, now known or hereafter invented, including photocopying and recording, or in any information storage or retrieval system, without permission in writing from the publishers.

Routledge is committed to publishing material that promotes the best in inquiry-based science education. However, conditions of actual use may vary, and the safety procedures and practices described in this book are intended to serve only as a guide. Additional precautionary measures may be required. Routledge and the authors do not warrant or represent that the procedures and practices in this book meet any safety code or standard of federal, state, or local regulations. Routledge and the authors disclaim any liability for personal injury or damage to property arising out of or relating to the use of this book, including any of the recommendations, instructions, or materials contained therein.

Trademark notice: Product or corporate names may be trademarks or registered trademarks, and are used only for identification and explanation without intent to infringe.

ISBN: 978-1-032-42344-9 (hbk)
ISBN: 978-1-032-42337-1 (pbk)
ISBN: 978-1-003-36237-1 (ebk)

DOI: 10.4324/9781003362371

Typeset in Palatino LT Std
by KnowledgeWorks Global Ltd.

CONTENTS

C⦿NTENTS

Part 2: Creating Global Bonds: STEM Road Map Module

③ How Students Learn in Grades 9–12 27

Erin Peters-Burton and Janet B. Walton

④ STEM Road Map Curriculum Module Overview 37

*Anthony Pellegrino, Jennifer Drake-Patrick, Brad Rankin,
Erin E. Peters-Burton, Janet B. Walton, and Carla C. Johnson*

CONTENTS

CONTENTS

CONTENTS

ABOUT THE EDITORS AND AUTHORS

Dr. Carla C. Johnson is a Professor of Science Education and Office of Research and Innovation Faculty Research Fellow at NC State University. Dr. Johnson has served (2015–2021) as the director of research and evaluation for the Department of Defense–funded Army Educational Outreach Program (AEOP), a global portfolio of STEM education programs, competitions, and apprenticeships. She has been a leader in STEM education for the past decade, serving as the director of STEM Centers, editor of the *School Science and Mathematics* journal, and lead researcher for the evaluation of Tennessee's Race to the Top–funded STEM portfolio. Dr. Johnson has published over 200 articles, books, book chapters, and curriculum books focused on STEM education. She is a former science and social studies teacher and was the recipient of the 2013 Outstanding Science Teacher Educator of the Year award from the Association for Science Teacher Education (ASTE), the 2012 Award for Excellence in Integrating Science and Mathematics from the School Science and Mathematics Association (SSMA), the 2014 award for best paper on Implications of Research for Educational Practice from ASTE, and the 2006 Outstanding Early Career Scholar Award from SSMA. Her research focuses on STEM education policy implementation, effective science teaching, and integrated STEM approaches.

Dr. Janet B. Walton is a Senior Research Scholar at NC State College of Education in Raleigh, North Carolina. Formerly the STEM workforce program manager for Virginia's Region 2000 and founding director of the Future Focus Foundation, a nonprofit organization dedicated to enhancing the quality of STEM education in the region, she merges her economic development and education backgrounds to develop K–12 curricular materials that integrate real-life issues with sound cross-curricular content. Her research focus includes collaboration between schools and community stakeholders for STEM education, problem- and project-based learning pedagogies, online learning, and mixed methods research methodologies. She leverages this background to bring contextual STEM experiences into the classroom and provide students and educators with innovative resources and curricular materials. She is the former assistant director of evaluation of research and evaluation for the Department of Defense–funded Army Educational Outreach Program (AEOP), a global portfolio of STEM education programs, competitions, and apprenticeships, and specializes in evaluation of STEM programs.

Dr. Erin E. Peters-Burton is the Donna R. and David E. Sterling Endowed Professor in Science Education at George Mason University in Fairfax, Virginia. She uses her experiences from 15 years as an engineer and secondary science, engineering, and mathematics teacher to develop research projects that directly inform classroom practice in science and engineering. Her research agenda is based on the idea that all students should build self-awareness of how they learn science and engineering. She works to help students see themselves as "science-minded" and help teachers create classrooms that support student skills to develop scientific knowledge. To accomplish this, she pursues research projects that investigate ways that students and teachers can use self-regulated learning theory in science and engineering, as well as how inclusive STEM schools can help students succeed. During her tenure as a secondary teacher, she had a National Board Certification in Early Adolescent Science and was an Albert Einstein Distinguished Educator Fellow for NASA. As a researcher, Dr. Peters-Burton has published over 100 articles, books, book chapters, and curriculum books focused on STEM education and educational psychology. She received the Outstanding Science Teacher Educator of the Year award from ASTE in 2016 and a Teacher of Distinction Award and a Scholarly Achievement Award from George Mason University in 2012, and in 2010 she was named University Science Educator of the Year by the Virginia Association of Science Teachers.

Dr. Jennifer Drake-Patrick is an assistant professor of literacy education in the College of Education and Human Development at George Mason University. A former English language arts teacher, she focuses her research on disciplinary literacy.

Dr. Toni A. May is an associate professor of assessment, research, and statistics in the School of Education at Drexel University in Philadelphia. Dr. May's research concentrates on assessment and evaluation in education, with a focus on K–12 STEM.

Dr. Tamara J. Moore is an associate professor of engineering education in the College of Engineering at Purdue University. Dr. Moore's research focuses on defining STEM integration through the use of engineering as the connection and investigating its power for student learning.

Dr. Anthony Pellegrino is an assistant professor of social science in the College of Education at The University of Tennessee, Knoxville. He is a former social studies and history teacher whose research interests include youth-centered pedagogies and social science teacher preparation.

Dr. Bradley D. Rankin is a high school mathematics teacher at Wakefield High School in Arlington, Virginia. He has been teaching mathematics for 20 years, is board certified, and has a PhD in mathematics education leadership from George Mason University.

ACKNOWLEDGEMENTS

This module was developed as a part of the STEM Road Map project (Carla C. Johnson, PI). The Purdue University College of Education, General Motors, and other sources provided funding for this project.

Copyright © 2015 from *STEM road map: A framework for integrated STEM education* by C. C. Johnson, E. E. Peters-Burton, & T. J. Moore (Eds.). Reproduced by permission of Taylor and Francis Group, LLC, a division of Informa plc.

See www.routledge.com/products/9781138804234 for more information about *STEM Road Map: A Framework for Integrated STEM Education.*

PART 1

THE STEM ROAD MAP

BACKGROUND, THEORY, AND PRACTICE

OVERVIEW OF THE *STEM ROAD MAP CURRICULUM SERIES*

Carla C. Johnson, Erin Peters-Burton, and Tamara J. Moore

The *STEM Road Map Curriculum Series* was conceptualized and developed by a team of STEM educators from across the United States in response to a growing need to infuse real-world learning contexts, delivered through authentic problem-solving pedagogy, into K–12 classrooms. The curriculum series is grounded in integrated STEM, which focuses on the integration of the STEM disciplines – science, technology, engineering, and mathematics – delivered across content areas, incorporating the Framework for 21st Century Learning along with grade-level-appropriate academic standards. The curriculum series begins in kindergarten, with a five-week instructional sequence that introduces students to the STEM themes and gives them grade-level-appropriate topics and real-world challenges or problems to solve. The series uses project-based and problem-based learning, presenting students with the problem or challenge during the first lesson, and then teaching them science, social studies, English language arts, mathematics, and other content, as they apply what they learn to the challenge or problem at hand.

Authentic assessment and differentiation are embedded throughout the modules. Each *STEM Road Map Curriculum Series* module has a lead discipline, which may be science, social studies, English language arts, or mathematics. All disciplines are integrated into each module, along with ties to engineering. Another key component is the use of STEM Research Notebooks to allow students to track their own learning progress. The modules are designed with a scaffolded approach, with increasingly complex concepts and skills introduced as students progress through grade levels.

The developers of this work view the curriculum as a resource that is intended to be used either as a whole or in part to meet the needs of districts, schools, and teachers who are implementing an integrated STEM approach. A variety of implementation formats are possible, from using one stand-alone module at a given grade level to using all five modules to provide 25 weeks of instruction. Also, within each grade

DOI: 10.4324/9781003362371-2

band (K–2, 3–5, 6–8, 9–12), the modules can be sequenced in various ways to suit specific needs.

STANDARDS-BASED APPROACH

The *STEM Road Map Curriculum Series* is anchored in the *Next Generation Science Standards* (*NGSS*), the *Common Core State Standards for Mathematics* (*CCSS Mathematics*), the *Common Core State Standards for English Language Arts* (*CCSS ELA*), and the Framework for 21st Century Learning. Each module includes a detailed curriculum map that incorporates the associated standards from the particular area correlated to lesson plans. The STEM Road Map has very clear and strong connections to these academic standards, and each of the grade-level topics was derived from the mapping of the standards to ensure alignment among topics, challenges or problems, and the required academic standards for students. Therefore, the curriculum series takes a standards-based approach and is designed to provide authentic contexts for application of required knowledge and skills.

THEMES IN THE *STEM ROAD MAP CURRICULUM SERIES*

The K–12 STEM Road Map is organized around five real-world STEM themes that were generated through an examination of the big ideas and challenges for society included in STEM standards and those that are persistent dilemmas for current and future generations:

- Cause and Effect
- Innovation and Progress
- The Represented World
- Sustainable Systems
- Optimizing the Human Experience

These themes are designed as springboards for launching students into an exploration of real-world learning situated within big ideas. Most important, the five STEM Road Map themes serve as a framework for scaffolding STEM learning across the K–12 continuum.

The themes are distributed across the STEM disciplines so that they represent the big ideas in science (Cause and Effect; Sustainable Systems), technology (Innovation and Progress; Optimizing the Human Experience), engineering (Innovation and Progress; Sustainable Systems; Optimizing the Human Experience), and mathematics (The Rep-resented World), as well as concepts and challenges in social studies and 21st century skills that are also excellent contexts for learning in English language arts. The process of developing themes began with the clustering of the *NGSS* performance expectations and the National Academy of Engineering's grand challenges for engineering, which led to the development of the challenge in each module and connections of the module activities to the *CCSS Mathematics* and *CCSS ELA* standards. We performed these mapping processes with large teams of experts and found that these five themes provided breadth, depth, and coherence to frame a high-quality STEM learning experience from kindergarten through 12th grade.

Cause and Effect

The concept of cause and effect is a powerful and pervasive notion in the STEM fields. It is the foundation of understanding how and why things happen as they do. Humans spend considerable effort and resources trying to understand the causes and effects of natural and designed phenomena to gain better control over events and the environment and to be prepared to react appropriately. Equipped with the knowledge of a specific cause-and-effect relationship, we can lead better lives or contribute to the community by altering the cause, leading to a different effect. For example, if a person recognizes that irresponsible energy consumption leads to global climate change, that person can act to remedy his or her contribution to the situation. Although cause and effect is a core idea in the STEM fields, it can actually be difficult to determine. Students should be capable of understanding not only when evidence points to cause and effect but also when evidence points to relationships but not direct causality. The major goal of education is to foster students to be empowered, analytic thinkers, capable of thinking through complex processes to make important decisions. Understanding causality, as well as when it cannot be determined, will help students become better consumers, global citizens, and community members.

Innovation and Progress

One of the most important factors in determining whether humans will have a positive future is innovation. Innovation is the driving force behind progress, which helps create possibilities that did not exist before. Innovation and progress are creative entities, but in the STEM fields, they are anchored by evidence and logic, and they use established concepts to move the STEM fields forward. In creating something new, students must consider what is already known in the STEM fields and apply this knowledge appropriately. When we innovate, we create value that was not there previously and create new conditions and possibilities for even more innovations. Students should consider how their innovations might affect progress and use their STEM thinking to change current human burdens to benefits. For example, if we develop more efficient cars that use by-products from another manufacturing industry, such as food processing, then we have used waste productively and reduced the need for the waste to be hauled away, an indirect benefit of the innovation.

The Represented World

When we communicate about the world we live in, how the world works, and how we can meet the needs of humans, sometimes we can use the actual phenomena to explain a concept. Sometimes, however, the concept is too big, too slow, too small, too fast, or too complex for us to explain using the actual phenomena, and we must use a representation or a model to help communicate the important features. We need representations and models such as graphs, tables, mathematical expressions, and diagrams because it makes our thinking visible. For example, when examining geologic time, we cannot actually observe the passage of such large chunks of time, so we create a timeline or a model that uses a proportional scale to visually illustrate how much time has passed for different eras. Another example may be something too complex for students at a particular grade level, such as explaining the p subshell orbitals of electrons to fifth graders. Instead, we use the Bohr model, which more closely represents the orbiting of planets and is accessible to fifth graders.

When we create models, they are helpful because they point out the most important features of a phenomenon. We also create representations of the world with mathematical functions, which help us change parameters to suit the situation. Creating representations of a phenomenon engages students because they are able to identify the important features of that phenomenon and communicate them directly. But because models are estimates of a phenomenon, they leave out some of the details, so it is important for students to evaluate their usefulness as well as their shortcomings.

Sustainable Systems

From an engineering perspective, the term *system* refers to the use of "concepts of component need, component interaction, systems interaction, and feedback. The interaction of subcomponents to produce a functional system is a common lens used by all engineering disciplines for understanding, analysis, and design" (Koehler et al., 2013, p. 8). Systems can be either open (e.g., an ecosystem) or closed (e.g., a car battery). Ideally, a system should be sustainable, able to maintain equilibrium without much energy from outside the structure. Looking at a garden, we see flowers blooming, weeds sprouting, insects buzzing, and various forms of life living within its boundaries. This is an example of an ecosystem, a collection of living organisms that survive together, functioning as a system. The interaction of the organisms within the system and the influences of the environment (e.g., water, sunlight) can maintain the system for a period of time, thus demonstrating its ability to endure. Sustainability is a desirable feature of a system because it allows for existence of the entity in the long term.

In the STEM Road Map project, we identified different standards that we consider to be oriented toward systems that students should know and understand in the K–12 setting. These include ecosystems, the rock cycle, Earth processes (such as erosion, tectonics, ocean currents, weather phenomena), Earth-Sun-Moon cycles, heat transfer, and the interaction among the geosphere, biosphere, hydrosphere, and atmosphere. Students and teachers should understand that we live in a world of systems that are not independent of each other, but rather are intrinsically linked such that a disruption in one part of a system will have reverberating effects on other parts of the system.

Optimizing the Human Experience

Science, technology, engineering, and mathematics as disciplines have the capacity to continuously improve the ways humans live, interact, and find meaning in the world, thus working to optimize the human experience. This idea has two components: being more suited to our environment and being more fully human. For example, the progression of STEM ideas can help humans create solutions to complex problems, such as improving ways to access water sources, designing energy sources with minimal impact on our environment, developing new ways of communication and expression, and building efficient shelters. STEM ideas can also provide access to the secrets and wonders of nature. Learning in STEM requires students to think logically and systematically, which is a way of knowing the world that is markedly different from knowing the world as an artist. When students can employ various ways of knowing and understand when it is appropriate to use a different way of knowing or integrate ways of knowing, they are fully experiencing the best of what it is to be human. The problem-based learning scenarios provided in the STEM Road Map help students develop ways of thinking like STEM professionals as they ask questions and design solutions. They learn to optimize the human experience by innovating improvements in the designed world in which they live.

THE NEED FOR AN INTEGRATED STEM APPROACH

At a basic level, STEM stands for science, technology, engineering, and mathematics. Over the past decade, however, STEM has evolved to have a much broader scope and implications. Now, educators and policy makers refer to STEM as not only a concentrated area for investing in the future of the United States and other nations but also as a domain and mechanism for educational reform.

The good intentions of the recent decade-plus of focus on accountability and increased testing has resulted in significant decreases not only in instructional time for teaching science and social studies but also in the flexibility of teachers to promote authentic, problem-solving–focused classroom environments. The shift has had a detrimental impact on student acquisition of vitally important skills, which many refer to as 21st century skills, and often the ability of students to "think." Further, schooling has become increasingly siloed into compartments of mathematics, science, English

language arts, and social studies, lacking any of the connections that are overwhelmingly present in the real world around children. Students have experienced school as content provided in boxes that must be memorized, devoid of any real-world context, and often have little understanding of why they are learning these things.

STEM-focused projects, curriculum, activities, and schools have emerged as a means to address these challenges. However, most of these efforts have continued to focus on the individual STEM disciplines (predominantly science and engineering) through more STEM classes and after-school programs in a "STEM-enhanced" approach (Breiner et al., 2012). But in traditional and STEM-enhanced approaches, there is little to no focus on other disciplines that are integral to the context of STEM in the real world. Integrated STEM education, on the other hand, infuses the learning of important STEM content and concepts with a much-needed emphasis on 21st century skills and a problem- and project-based pedagogy that more closely mirrors the real-world setting for society's challenges. It incorporates social studies, English language arts, and the arts as pivotal and necessary (Johnson, 2013; Rennie et al., 2012; Roehrig et al., 2012).

FRAMEWORK FOR STEM INTEGRATION IN THE CLASSROOM

The *STEM Road Map Curriculum Series* is grounded in the Framework for STEM Integration in the Classroom as conceptualized by Moore, Guzey, and Brown (2014) and Moore et al. (2014). The framework has six elements, described in the context of how they are used in the *STEM Road Map Curriculum Series* as follows:

1. The STEM Road Map contexts are meaningful to students and provide motivation to engage with the content. Together, these allow students to have different ways to enter into the challenge.

2. The STEM Road Map modules include engineering design that allows students to design technologies (i.e., products that are part of the designed world) for a compelling purpose.

3. The STEM Road Map modules provide students with the opportunities to learn from failure and redesign based on the lessons learned.

4. The STEM Road Map modules include standards-based disciplinary content as the learning objectives.

5. The STEM Road Map modules include student-centered pedagogies that allow students to grapple with the content, tie their ideas to the context, and learn to think for themselves as they deepen their conceptual knowledge.

6. The STEM Road Map modules emphasize 21st century skills and, in particular, highlight communication and teamwork.

All of the STEM Road Map modules incorporate these six elements; however, the level of emphasis on each of these elements varies based on the challenge or problem in each module.

THE NEED FOR THE *STEM ROAD MAP CURRICULUM SERIES*

As focus is increasing on integrated STEM, and additional schools and programs decide to move their curriculum and instruction in this direction, there is a need for high-quality, research-based curriculum designed with integrated STEM at the core. Several good resources are available to help teachers infuse engineering or more STEM-enhanced approaches, but no curriculum exists that spans K–12 with an integrated STEM focus. The next chapter provides detailed information about the specific pedagogy, instructional strategies, and learning theory on which the *STEM Road Map Curriculum Series* is grounded.

REFERENCES

Breiner, J., Harkness, M., Johnson, C. C., & Koehler, C. (2012). What is STEM? A discussion about conceptions of STEM in education and partnerships. *School Science and Mathematics, 112*(1), 3–11.

Johnson, C. C. (2013). Conceptualizing integrated STEM education: Editorial. *School Science and Mathematics, 113*(8), 367–368.

Koehler, C. M., Bloom, M. A., & Binns, I. C. (2013). Lights, camera, action: Developing a methodology to document mainstream films' portrayal of nature of science and scientific inquiry. *Electronic Journal of Science Education, 17*(2).

Moore, T. J., Guzey, S. S., & Brown, A. (2014). Greenhouse design to increase habitable land: An engineering unit. *Science Scope, 37*(7), 51–57.

Moore, T. J., Stohlmann, M. S., Wang, H.-H., Tank, K. M., Glancy, A. W., & Roehrig, G. H. (2014). Implementation and integration of engineering in K–12 STEM education. In S. Purzer, J. Strobel, & M. Cardella (Eds.), *Engineering in pre-college settings: Synthesizing research, policy, and practices* (pp. 35–60). Purdue Press.

Rennie, L., Venville, G., & Wallace, J. (2012). *Integrating science, technology, engineering, and mathematics: Issues, reflections, and ways forward.* Routledge.

Roehrig, G. H., Moore, T. J., Wang, H. H., & Park, M. S. (2012). Is adding the E enough? Investigating the impact of K–12 engineering standards on the implementation of STEM integration. *School Science and Mathematics, 112*(1), 31–44.

STRATEGIES USED IN THE *STEM ROAD MAP CURRICULUM SERIES*

Erin Peters-Burton, Carla C. Johnson, Toni A. May, and Tamara J. Moore

The *STEM Road Map Curriculum Series* uses what has been identified through research as best-practice pedagogy, including embedded formative assessment strategies throughout each module. This chapter briefly describes the key strategies that are employed in the series.

PROJECT- AND PROBLEM-BASED LEARNING

Each module in the *STEM Road Map Curriculum Series* uses either project-based learning or problem-based learning to drive the instruction. Project-based learning begins with a driving question to guide student teams in addressing a contextualized local or community problem or issue. The outcome of project-based instruction is a product that is conceptualized, designed, and tested through a series of scaffolded learning experiences (Blumenfeld et al., 1991; Krajcik & Blumenfeld, 2006). Problem-based learning is often grounded in a fictitious scenario, challenge, or problem (Barell, 2006; Lambros, 2004). On the first day of instruction within the unit, student teams are provided with the context of the problem. Teams work through a series of activities and use open-ended research to develop their potential solution to the problem or challenge, which need not be a tangible product (Johnson, 2003).

ENGINEERING DESIGN PROCESS

The *STEM Road Map Curriculum Series* uses engineering design as a way to facilitate integrated STEM within the modules. The engineering design process (EDP) is depicted in Figure 2.1 (p. 12). It highlights two major aspects of engineering design – problem scoping and solution generation – and six specific components of working

DOI: 10.4324/9781003362371-3

Figure 2.1. Engineering Design Process

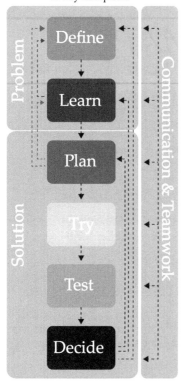

Engineering Design Process
A way to improve

Copyright © 2015 PictureSTEM, Purdue University Research Foundation

toward a design: define the problem, learn about the problem, plan a solution, try the solution, test the solution, decide whether the solution is good enough. It also shows that communication and teamwork are involved throughout the entire process. As the arrows in the figure indicate, the order in which the components of engineering design are addressed depends on what becomes needed as designers progress through the EDP. Designers must communicate and work in teams throughout the process. The EDP is iterative, meaning that components of the process can be repeated as needed until the design is good enough to present to the client as a potential solution to the problem.

Problem scoping is the process of gathering and analyzing information to deeply understand the engineering design problem. It includes defining the problem and learning about the problem. Defining the problem includes identifying the problem, the client, and the end user of the design. The client is the person (or people) who hired the designers to do the work, and the end user is the person (or people) who will use the final design. The designers must also identify the criteria and the constraints of the problem. The criteria are the things the client wants from the solution, and the constraints are the things that limit the possible solutions. The designers must spend significant time learning about the problem, which can include activities such as the following:

- Reading informational texts and researching about relevant concepts or contexts

- Identifying and learning about needed mathematical and scientific skills, knowledge, and tools

- Learning about things done previously to solve similar problems

- Experimenting with possible materials that could be used in the design

Problem scoping also allows designers to consider how to measure the success of the design in addressing specific criteria and staying within the constraints over multiple iterations of solution generation.

Solution generation includes planning a solution, trying the solution, testing the solution, and deciding whether the solution is good enough. Planning the solution includes generating many design ideas that both address the criteria and meet the constraints.

Here the designers must consider what was learned about the problem during problem scoping. Design plans include clear communication of design ideas through media such as notebooks, blueprints, schematics, or storyboards. They also include details about the design, such as measurements, materials, colors, costs of materials, instructions for how things fit together, and sets of directions. Making the decision about which design idea to move forward involves considering the trade-offs of each design idea.

Once a clear design plan is in place, the designers must try the solution. Trying the solution includes developing a prototype (a testable model) based on the plan generated. The prototype might be something physical or a process to accomplish a goal. This component of design requires that the designers consider the risk involved in implementing the design. The prototype developed must be tested. Testing the solution includes conducting fair tests that verify whether the plan is a solution that is good enough to meet the client and end user needs and wants. Data need to be collected about the results of the tests of the prototype, and these data should be used to make evidence-based decisions regarding the design choices made in the plan. Here, the designers must again consider the criteria and constraints for the problem.

Using the data gathered from the testing, the designers must decide whether the solution is good enough to meet the client and end user needs and wants by assessment based on the criteria and constraints. Here, the designers must justify or reject design decisions based on the background research gathered while learning about the problem and on the evidence gathered during the testing of the solution. The designers must now decide whether to present the current solution to the client as a possibility or to do more iterations of design on the solution. If they decide that improvements need to be made to the solution, the designers must decide if there is more that needs to be understood about the problem, client, or end user; if another design idea should be tried; or if more planning needs to be conducted on the same design. One way or another, more work needs to be done.

Throughout the process of designing a solution to meet a client's needs and wants, designers work in teams and must communicate to each other, the client, and likely the end user. Teamwork is important in engineering design because multiple perspectives and differing skills and knowledge are valuable when working to solve problems. Communication is key to the success of the designed solution. Designers must communicate their ideas clearly using many different representations, such as text in an engineering notebook, diagrams, flowcharts, technical briefs, or memos to the client.

LEARNING CYCLE

The same format for the learning cycle is used in all grade levels throughout the STEM Road Map, so that students engage in a variety of activities to learn about phenomena in the modules thoroughly and have consistent experiences in the problem- and project- based learning modules. Expectations for learning by younger students are

not as high as for older students, but the format of the progression of learning is the same. Students who have learned with curriculum from the STEM Road Map in early grades know what to expect in later grades. The learning cycle consists of five parts – Introductory Activity/Engagement, Activity/Exploration, Explanation, Elaboration/Application of Knowledge, and Evaluation/Assessment – and is based on the empirically tested 5E model from BSCS (Bybee et al., 2006).

In the Introductory Activity/Engagement phase, teachers introduce the module challenge and use a unique approach designed to pique students' curiosity. This phase gets students to start thinking about what they already know about the topic and begin wondering about key ideas. The Introductory Activity/Engagement phase positions students to be confident about what they are about to learn, because they have prior knowledge, and clues them into what they don't yet know.

In the Activity/Exploration phase, the teacher sets up activities in which students experience a deeper look at the topics that were introduced earlier. Students engage in the activities and generate new questions or consider possibilities using preliminary investigations. Students work independently, in small groups, and in whole-group settings to conduct investigations, resulting in common experiences about the topic and skills involved in the real-world activities. Teachers can assess students' development of concepts and skills based on the common experiences during this phase.

During the Explanation phase, teachers direct students' attention to concepts they need to understand and skills they need to possess to accomplish the challenge. Students participate in activities to demonstrate their knowledge and skills to this point, and teachers can pinpoint gaps in student knowledge during this phase.

In the Elaboration/Application of Knowledge phase, teachers present students with activities that engage in higher-order thinking to create depth and breadth of student knowledge, while connecting ideas across topics within and across STEM. Students apply what they have learned thus far in the module to a new context or elaborate on what they have learned about the topic to a deeper level of detail.

In the last phase, Evaluation/Assessment, teachers give students summative feedback on their knowledge and skills as demonstrated through the challenge. This is not the only point of assessment (as discussed in the section on Embedded Formative Assessments), but it is an assessment of the culmination of the knowledge and skills for the module. Students demonstrate their cognitive growth at this point and reflect on how far they have come since the beginning of the module. The challenges are designed to be multidimensional in the ways students must collaborate and communicate their new knowledge.

STEM RESEARCH NOTEBOOK

One of the main components of the *STEM Road Map Curriculum Series* is the STEM Research Notebook, a place for students to capture their ideas, questions, observations, reflections, evidence of progress, and other items associated with their daily work. At the beginning of each module, the teacher walks students through the setup of the STEM Research Notebook, which could be a three-ring binder, composition book, or spiral notebook. You may wish to have students create divided sections so that they can easily access work from various disciplines during the module. Electronic notebooks kept on student devices are also acceptable and encouraged. Students will develop their own table of contents and create chapters in the notebook for each module.

Each lesson in the *STEM Road Map Curriculum Series* includes one or more prompts that are designed for inclusion in the STEM Research Notebook and appear as questions or statements that the teacher assigns to students. These prompts require students to apply what they have learned across the lesson to solve the big problem or challenge for that module. Each lesson is designed to meaningfully refer students to the larger problem or challenge they have been assigned to solve with their teams. The STEM Research Notebook is designed to be a key formative assessment tool, as students' daily entries provide evidence of what they are learning. The notebook can be used as a mechanism for dialogue between the teacher and students, as well as for peer and self-evaluation.

The use of the STEM Research Notebook is designed to scaffold student notebooking skills across the grade bands in the *STEM Road Map Curriculum Series*. In the early grades, children learn how to organize their daily work in the notebook as a way to collect their products for future reference. In elementary school, students structure their notebooks to integrate background research along with their daily work and lesson prompts. In the upper grades (middle and high school), students expand their use of research and data gathering through team discussions to more closely mirror the work of STEM experts in the real world.

THE ROLE OF ASSESSMENT IN THE *STEM ROAD MAP CURRICULUM SERIES*

Starting in the middle years and continuing into secondary education, the word *assessment* typically brings grades to mind. These grades may take the form of a letter or a percentage, but they typically are used as a representation of a student's content mastery. If well thought out and implemented, however, classroom assessment can offer teachers, parents, and students valuable information about student learning and misconceptions that does not necessarily come in the form of a grade (Popham, 2013).

The *STEM Road Map Curriculum Series* provides a set of assessments for each module. Teachers are encouraged to use assessment information for more than just assigning grades to students. Instead, assessments of activities requiring students to actively engage in their learning, such as student journaling in STEM Research Notebooks, collaborative presentations, and constructing graphic organizers, should be used to move student learning forward. Whereas other curriculum with assessments may include

objective-type (multiple-choice or matching) tests, quizzes, or worksheets, we have intentionally avoided these forms of assessments to better align assessment strategies with teacher instruction and student learning techniques. Since the focus of this book is on project- or problem-based STEM curriculum and instruction that focuses on higher-level thinking skills, appropriate and authentic performance assessments were developed to elicit the most reliable and valid indication of growth in student abilities (Brookhart & Nitko, 2008).

Comprehensive Assessment System

Assessment throughout all STEM Road Map curriculum modules acts as a comprehensive system in which formative and summative assessments work together to provide teachers with high-quality information on student learning. Formative assessment occurs when the teacher finds out formally or informally what a student knows about a smaller, defined concept or skill and provides timely feedback to the student about his or her level of proficiency. Summative assessments occur when students have performed all activities in the module and are given a cumulative performance evaluation in which they demonstrate their growth in learning.

A comprehensive assessment system can be thought of as akin to a sporting event. Formative assessments are the practices: It is important to accomplish them consistently, they provide feedback to help students improve their learning, and making mistakes can be worthwhile if students are given an opportunity to learn from them. Summative assessments are the competitions: Students need to be prepared to perform at the best of their ability. Without multiple opportunities to practice skills along the way through formative assessments, students will not have the best chance of demonstrating growth in abilities through summative assessments (Black & Wiliam, 1998).

Embedded Formative Assessments

Formative assessments in this module serve two main purposes: to provide feedback to students about their learning and to provide important information for the teacher to inform immediate instructional needs. Providing feedback to students is particularly important when conducting problem- or project-based learning because students take on much of the responsibility for learning, and teachers must facilitate student learning in an informed way. For example, if students are required to conduct research for the Activity/Exploration phase but are not familiar with what constitutes a reliable resource, they may develop misconceptions based on poor information. When a teacher monitors this learning through formative assessments and provides specific feedback related to the instructional goals, students are less likely to develop incomplete or incorrect conceptions in their independent investigations. By using formative assessment to detect problems in student learning and then

acting on this information, teachers help move student learning forward through these teachable moments.

Formative assessments come in a variety of formats. They can be informal, such as asking students probing questions related to student knowledge or tasks or simply observing students engaged in an activity to gather information about student skills. Formative assessments can also be formal, such as a written quiz or a laboratory practical. Regardless of the type, three key steps must be completed when using formative assessments (Sondergeld et al., 2010). First, the assessment is delivered to students so that teachers can collect data. Next, teachers analyze the data (student responses) to determine student strengths and areas that need additional support. Finally, teachers use the results from information collected to modify lessons and create learning environments that reinforce weak points in student learning. If student learning information is not used to modify instruction, the assessment cannot be considered formative in nature. Formative assessments can be about content, science process skills, or even learning skills. When a formative assessment focuses on content, it assesses student knowledge about the disciplinary core ideas from the *Next Generation Science Standards* (*NGSS*) or content objectives from *Common Core State Standards for Mathematics* (*CCSS Mathematics*) or *Common Core State Standards for English Language Arts* (*CCSS ELA*). Content-focused formative assessments ask students questions about declarative knowledge regarding the concepts they have been learning. Process skills formative assessments examine the extent to which a student can perform science and engineering practices from the *NGSS* or process objectives from *CCSS Mathematics* or *CCSS ELA*, such as constructing an argument. Learning skills can also be assessed formatively by asking students to reflect on the ways they learn best during a module and identify ways they could have learned more.

Assessment Maps

Assessment maps or blueprints can be used to ensure alignment between classroom instruction and assessment. If what students are learning in the classroom is not the same as the content on which they are assessed, the resultant judgment made on student learning will be invalid (Brookhart & Nitko, 2008). Therefore, the issue of instruction and assessment alignment is critical. The assessment map for this book (found in Chapter 3) indicates by lesson whether the assessment should be completed as a group or on an individual basis, identifies the assessment as formative or summative in nature, and aligns the assessment with its corresponding learning objectives.

Note that the module includes far more formative assessments than summative assessments. This is done intentionally to provide students with multiple opportunities to practice their learning of new skills before completing a summative assessment. Note also that formative assessments are used to collect information on only one or two learning objectives at a time so that potential relearning or instructional

modifications can focus on smaller and more manageable chunks of information. Conversely, summative assessments in the module cover many more learning objectives, as they are traditionally used as final markers of student learning. This is not to say that information collected from summative assessments cannot or should not be used formatively. If teachers find that gaps in student learning persist after a summative assessment is completed, it is important to revisit these existing misconceptions or areas of weakness before moving on (Black et al., 2003).

SELF-REGULATED LEARNING THEORY IN THE STEM ROAD MAP MODULES

Many learning theories are compatible with the STEM Road Map modules, such as constructivism, situated cognition, and meaningful learning. However, we feel that the self-regulated learning theory (SRL) aligns most appropriately (Zimmerman, 2000). SRL requires students to understand that thinking needs to be motivated and managed (Ritchhart et al., 2011). The STEM Road Map modules are student centered and are designed to provide students with choices, concrete hands-on experiences, and opportunities to see and make connections, especially across subjects (Eliason & Jenkins, 2012; NAEYC, 2016). Additionally, SRL is compatible with the modules because it fosters a learning environment that supports students' motivation, enables students to become aware of their own learning strategies, and requires reflection on learning while experiencing the module (Peters & Kitsantas, 2010).

Figure 2.2. SRL Theory

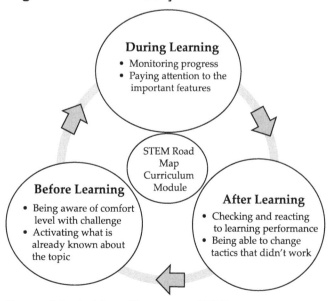

Source: Adapted from Zimmerman (2000).

The theory behind SRL (see Figure 2.2) explains the different processes that students engage in before, during, and after a learning task. Because SRL is a cyclical learning process, the accomplishment of one cycle develops strategies for the next learning cycle. This cyclic way of learning aligns with the various sections in the STEM Road Map lesson plans on Introductory Activity/Engagement, Activity/Exploration, Explanation, Elaboration/Application of Knowledge, and Evaluation/Assessment. Since the students engaged in a module take on much of the responsibility for learning, this theory also provides guidance for teachers to keep students on the right track.

The remainder of this section explains how SRL theory is embedded within the five sections of each module and points out ways to support students in becoming independent learners of STEM while productively functioning in collaborative teams.

Before Learning: Setting the Stage

Before attempting a learning task such as the STEM Road Map modules, teachers should develop an understanding of their students' level of comfort with the process of accomplishing the learning and determine what they already know about the topic. When students are comfortable with attempting a learning task, they tend to take more risks in learning and as a result achieve deeper learning (Bandura, 1986).

The STEM Road Map curriculum modules are designed to foster excitement from the very beginning. Each module has an Introductory Activity/Engagement section that introduces the overall topic from a unique and exciting perspective, engaging the students to learn more so that they can accomplish the challenge. The Introductory Activity also has a design component that helps teachers assess what students already know about the topic of the module. In addition to the deliberate designs in the lesson plans to support SRL, teachers can support a high level of student comfort with the learning challenge by finding out if students have ever accomplished the same kind of task and, if so, asking them to share what worked well for them.

During Learning: Staying the Course

Some students fear inquiry learning because they aren't sure what to do to be successful (Peters, 2010). However, the STEM Road Map curriculum modules are embedded with tools to help students pay attention to knowledge and skills that are important for the learning task and to check student understanding along the way. One of the most important processes for learning is the ability for learners to monitor their own progress while performing a learning task (Peters, 2012). The modules allow students to monitor their progress with tools such as the STEM Research Notebooks, in which they record what they know and can check whether they have acquired a complete set of knowledge and skills. The STEM Road Map modules support inquiry strategies that include previewing, questioning, predicting, clarifying, observing, discussing, and journaling (Morrison & Milner, 2014). Through the use of technology throughout the modules, inquiry is supported by providing students access to resources and data while enabling them to process information, report the findings, collaborate, and develop 21st century skills.

It is important for teachers to encourage students to have an open mind about alternative solutions and procedures (Milner & Sondergeld, 2015) when working through the STEM Road Map curriculum modules. Novice learners can have difficulty knowing what to pay attention to and tend to treat each possible avenue for information

as equal (Benner, 1984). Teachers are the mentors in a classroom and can point out ways for students to approach learning during the Activity/Exploration, Explanation, and Elaboration/Application of Knowledge portions of the lesson plans to ensure that students pay attention to the important concepts and skills throughout the module. For example, if a student is to demonstrate conceptual awareness of motion when working on roller coaster research, but the student has misconceptions about motion, the teacher can step in and redirect student learning.

After Learning: Knowing What Works

The classroom is a busy place, and it may often seem that there is no time for self-reflection on learning. Although skipping this reflective process may save time in the short term, it reduces the ability to take into account things that worked well and things that didn't so that teaching the module may be improved next time. In the long run, SRL skills are critical for students to become independent learners who can adapt to new situations. By investing the time it takes to teach students SRL skills, teachers can save time later, because students will be able to apply methods and approaches for learning that they have found effective to new situations. In the Evaluation/Assessment portion of the STEM Road Map curriculum modules, as well as in the formative assessments throughout the modules, two processes in the after-learning phase are supported: evaluating one's own performance and accounting for ways to adapt tactics that didn't work well. Students have many opportunities to self-assess in formative assessments, both in groups and individually, using the rubrics provided in the modules.

The designs of the *NGSS* and *CCSS* allow for students to learn in diverse ways, and the STEM Road Map curriculum modules emphasize that students can use a variety of tactics to complete the learning process. For example, students can use STEM Research Notebooks to record what they have learned during the various research activities. Notebook entries might include putting objectives in students' own words, compiling their prior learning on the topic, documenting new learning, providing proof of what they learned, and reflecting on what they felt successful doing and what they felt they still needed to work on. Perhaps students didn't realize that they were supposed to connect what they already knew with what they learned. They could record this and would be prepared in the next learning task to begin connecting prior learning with new learning.

SAFETY IN STEM

Student safety is a primary consideration in all subjects but is an area of particular concern in science, where students may interact with unfamiliar tools and materials that may pose additional safety risks. It is important to implement safety practices within the context of STEM investigations, whether in a classroom laboratory or in the field. When you keep safety in mind as a teacher, you avoid many potential issues with the lesson while also protecting your students.

STEM safety practices encompass things considered in the typical science classroom. Ensure that students are familiar with basic safety considerations, such as wearing protective equipment (e.g., safety glasses or goggles and latex-free gloves) and taking care with sharp objects, and know emergency exit procedures. Teachers should learn beforehand the locations of the safety eyewash, fume hood, fire extinguishers, and emergency shut-off switch in the classroom and how to use them. Also be aware of any school or district safety policies that are in place and apply those that align with the work being conducted in the lesson. It is important to review all safety procedures annually.

STEM investigations should always be supervised. Each lesson in the modules includes teacher guidelines for applicable safety procedures that should be followed. Before each investigation, teachers should go over these safety procedures with the student teams. Some STEM focus areas such as engineering require that students can demonstrate how to properly use equipment in the maker space before the teacher allows them to proceed with the lesson.

Information about classroom science safety, including a safety checklist for science classrooms, general lab safety recommendations, and links to other science safety resources, is available at the Council of State Science Supervisors (CSSS) website at www.cosss.org/Safety-Resources. The National Science Teachers Association (NSTA) provides a list of science rules and regulations, including standard operating procedures for lab safety, and a safety acknowledgement form for students and parents or guardians to sign. You can access these resources at http://static.nsta.org/pdfs/ SafetyInTheScienceClassroom.pdf. In addition, NSTA's Safety in the Science Classroom web page (*www.nsta.org/safety*) has numerous links to safety resources, including papers written by the NSTA Safety Advisory Board.

Disclaimer: The safety precautions for each activity are based on use of the recommended materials and instructions, legal safety standards, and better professional practices. Using alternative materials or procedures for these activities may jeopardize the level of safety and therefore is at the user's own risk.

REFERENCES

Bandura, A. (1986). *Social foundations of thought and action: A social cognitive theory.* Prentice-Hall.

Barell, J. (2006). *Problem-based learning: An inquiry approach.* Corwin Press.

Benner, P. (1984). *From novice to expert: Excellence and power in clinical nursing practice.* Addison-Wesley Publishing Company.

Black, P., Harrison, C., Lee, C., Marshall, B., & Wiliam, D. (2003). *Assessment for learning: Putting it into practice*. Open University Press.

Black, P., & Wiliam, D. (1998). Inside the black box: Raising standards through classroom assessment. *Phi Delta Kappan, 80*(2), 139–148.

Blumenfeld, P., Soloway, E., Marx, R., Krajcik, J., Guzdial, M., & Palincsar, A. (1991). Motivating project-based learning: Sustaining the doing, supporting learning. *Educational Psychologist, 26*(3), 369–398.

Brookhart, S. M., & Nitko, A. J. (2008). *Assessment and grading in classrooms*. Pearson.

Bybee, R., Taylor, J., Gardner, A., Scotter, P., Carlson, J., Westbrook, A., & Landes, N. (2006). *The BSCS 5E instructional model: Origins and effectiveness*.

Eliason, C. F., & Jenkins, L. T. (2012). *A practical guide to early childhood curriculum* (9th ed.). Merrill.

Johnson, C. (2003). Bioterrorism is real-world science: Inquiry-based simulation mirrors real life. *Science Scope, 27*(3), 19–23.

Krajcik, J., & Blumenfeld, P. (2006). Project-based learning. In R. K. Sawyer (Ed.), *The Cambridge handbook of the learning sciences* (pp. 317–334). Cambridge University Press.

Lambros, A. (2004). *Problem-based learning in middle and high school classrooms: A teacher's guide to implementation*. Corwin Press.

Milner, A. R., & Sondergeld, T. (2015). Gifted urban middle school students: The inquiry continuum and the nature of science. *National Journal of Urban Education and Practice, 8*(3), 442–461.

Morrison, V., & Milner, A. R. (2014). Literacy in support of science: A closer look at cross-curricular instructional practice. *Michigan Reading Journal, 46*(2), 42–56.

National Association for the Education of Young Children (NAEYC). (2016). *Developmentally appropriate practice position statements*. www.naeyc.org/positionstatements/dap.

Peters, E. E. (2010). Shifting to a student-centered science classroom: An exploration of teacher and student changes in perceptions and practices. *Journal of Science Teacher Education, 21*(3), 329–349.

Peters, E. E. (2012). Developing content knowledge in students through explicit teaching of the nature of science: Influences of goal setting and self-monitoring. *Science and Education, 21*(6), 881–898.

Peters, E. E., & Kitsantas, A. (2010). The effect of nature of science metacognitive prompts on science students' content and nature of science knowledge, metacognition, and self-regulatory efficacy. *School Science and Mathematics, 110*(8), 382–396.

Popham, W. J. (2013). *Classroom assessment: What teachers need to know* (7th ed.). Pearson.

Ritchhart, R., Church, M., & Morrison, K. (2011). *Making thinking visible: How to promote engagement, understanding, and independence for all learners*. Jossey-Bass.

Sondergeld, T. A., Bell, C. A., & Leusner, D. M. (2010). Understanding how teachers engage in formative assessment. *Teaching and Learning*, 24(2), 72–86.

Zimmerman, B. J. (2000). Attaining self-regulation: A social-cognitive perspective. In M. Boekaerts, P. Pintrich, & M. Zeidner (Eds.), *Handbook of self-regulation* (pp. 13–39). Academic Press.

PART 2

CREATING GLOBAL BONDS
STEM ROAD MAP MODULE

HOW STUDENTS LEARN
IN GRADES 9–12

Erin Peters-Burton and Janet B. Walton

In this chapter, we describe the foundational learning theory for the *STEM Road Map Curriculum Series* – with specific detail on grades 9–12 and the Car Crashes module. The STEM Road Map curriculum utilizes an integrated, problem and project-based approach, which can be a bit complex to teach, and often requires teachers to make timely decisions about structuring the learning environment. Therefore, having an understanding of the learning theory behind the activities in the STEM Road Map curriculum modules, including a focus on how students learn, will help teachers make important decisions about instruction (i.e., student research, explorations, investigations, and communication of results).

LEARNING IN GRADES 9–12

High school students are increasingly capable of understanding relationships between concepts, have more capacity to be strategic in their thinking, and are able to test hypotheses systematically (Harold et al., 2007). The STEM Road Map responds to these developmental changes by giving the students more responsibility for learning in the high school series. However, without supervision and guidance, students may not engage in proactive learning or they may not be familiar with the nature of scientific thinking, so they may not be able to act like a scientist initially (Hogan, 2000; Peters & Kitsantas, 2010). The modules in the STEM Road Map are created so that teachers can support students who need additional help. For example, when researching about how to construct a scale drawing of a car crash scene, more advanced students can find their own reliable resources, while other students may receive a short list of useful websites so that they do not launch their ideas from poor information.

LEARNING THEORY USED IN STEM ROAD MAP

Several learning theories are relevant to the STEM Road Map curriculum modules, including constructivism, situated cognition, and meaningful learning. Constructivism is a philosophical explanation for learning, and explains learning as the ability

DOI: 10.4324/9781003362371-5

for learners to create their own learning. Knowledge is not thrust upon learners in constructivism, but learners put together their own meaning of the world around them through their beliefs and experiences (Geary, 1995). Although constructivism is student centered, which is important in the STEM Road Map curriculum, it does not fully address the specific processes students use to construct knowledge nor ways teachers can intervene. Situated cognition is related to constructivism, in that it views the learning process to be an individual experience, but in addition claims that knowledge accrues through the lived practices of people in a society (Lemke, 1997). Situated cognition explains that learning occurs in communities of practice where people begin as novices and acquire more expertise, which does occur often in the STEM Road Map modules, but this theory does not take into account the reflective nature of the module design. Meaningful learning, originated by David Ausubel in 1963, views learning as ways learners can input new information and experiences, organize them hierarchically, and retain them. This theory has more detail about the processes of learning than constructivism and is student centered, but it does not explain how students might reflect on their learning to improve in the future.

Although these theories may have explanatory power with other contexts, the central theory used in our development of the STEM Road Map modules was Self-Regulated Learning Theory (SRL; Zimmerman, 2000) because of the student-centered, collaborative, reflective, and integrated design. SRL theory demonstrates that students learn most effectively when they are actively engaged in their learning environment and are aware of their own learning strategies. SRL encourages students to take greater responsibility for, reflect upon, and evaluate their own learning. The use of SRL strategies have been quite successful in improving student learning when used in a variety of subjects and settings (Bembenutty et al., 2013). For example, research has shown that teaching with SRL has helped students improve their learning about writing persuasive essays (Zimmerman & Kitsantas, 2002), solving problems in mathematics (Cheema & Kitsantas, 2013), and using scientific thinking in guided inquiry experiences (Peters & Kitsantas, 2010).

SRL theory is helpful in improving student learning in many different areas because it takes into account the tactics people employ when they approach a learning task, both in terms of what they already know and can do, and their beliefs about their own learning. SRL skills are not innate traits; any learner who becomes aware of their learning strategies can understand how to improve them (Zimmerman, 2000). Using SRL skills, therefore, all students can learn how to become better learners and put those skills into practice. This curriculum helps to support students in setting goals for learning and plans to reach those goals by introducing the final product at the beginning of the curriculum so that students can understand what they need to know along the way. There are also places for students to obtain feedback to monitor their progress. The STEM Road Map curriculum also helps students to reflect and improve on their work by giving them changes to revise, particularly with the final product from the challenge.

Not only does SRL explain the multidimensional ways in which people approach learning, but it also explains the different processes that people engage in before, during, and after a learning task. Figure 3.1 shows the different kinds of processes that will be discussed in this chapter and when they happen in terms of before, during, and after a learning task. Because SRL is a cycle, the learning strategies developed in one cycle carry over into subsequent learning cycles, resulting in an ever-increasing understanding and refinement of our own learning strategies. Although these processes are ultimately internal and driven by the learner, teachers can create environments for learning that can enhance these processes. For example, teachers can begin lessons with discrepant event demonstrations, which elicit prior knowledge and motivation from students. Teachers can also demonstrate to students what the most important ideas are in the lesson so that students are not distracted by extraneous information. Providing timely and specific feedback is also a way that teachers can enhance student learning.

Figure 3.1. SRL Theory

During Learning
- Monitoring progress
- Paying attention to the important features

STEM Road Map Curriculum Module

Before Learning
- Being aware of comfort level with challenge
- Activating what is already known about the topic

After Learning
- Checking and reacting to learning performance
- Being able to change tactics that didn't work

This way of looking at how people learn and how to help support learning undergirds the structure of the STEM Road Map curriculum modules, and aligns to the various sections in the lesson plans on Introductory Activity/Engagement, Activity/Investigation, Explanation, Extension/Application, and Assessment. Since the students engaged in a STEM Road Map curriculum module are challenged to take responsibility for learning, this theory also provides guidance for teachers to keep students on the right track.

In order to help better understand how SRL theory can help teachers support students, we will provide two student examples: Josie, who possesses poor SRL skills, and Miranda, who demonstrates positive SRL skills. Josie's teacher believes Josie has as much aptitude as any other student in her class, but notices that Josie is often quiet and passive when in a lab group and has poor awareness of her own skills. Josie is often confused because she thinks she does well on assignments, but usually gets a poor grade. For example, when given a design project for a new small animal enclosure for the zoo, Josie tries to motivate herself by saying "I haven't done well on these in the past, but this time is going to be different." Instead of making a plan to divide this long-term project into smaller tasks, Josie just mentally commits to finishing it in time. She spends small amounts of time working on the project, but

gets frustrated and works on other subjects instead or listens to music, ignoring that she hasn't accomplished anything. When she gets a low grade on the project with feedback about missing pieces, she just rolls her eyes, shoves the work in her backpack, and says to her friend, "I'm just not good at this stuff." The next time Josie is given a design challenge, she is even less motivated to proceed than she was with the prior challenge.

On the other hand, Miranda has the same ability level as Josie, but she employs better SRL skills than Josie. As soon as Miranda gets the same design assignment, she uses her calendar to plot out the due dates of pieces of work that will lead to the final product and meets with her groupmates to discuss and agree on a plan. Miranda then approaches her teacher with clarification questions about the products that are due and the types of feedback she'll get from the teacher. She then proactively plans independent time to do individual work and plans with the group to work together in a place where they will not be distracted. When Miranda meets a challenge in her research, she first approaches other students who are working on the same topic and asks them their strategies and, if that is not helpful, she approaches her teacher for support. When Miranda receives feedback on her project, she categorizes what worked for her and what didn't work for her, noting things that she has done before and confirming that they helped her accomplish the challenge. She looks at the things she could have improved and makes a note about what she might do better in the future, and if she cannot think of a new strategy, she approaches people who might be able to help her. She mentally celebrates what she did well, but doesn't beat herself up about the things she did not do well. Instead, she reflects on how she can change them next time and makes a tangible plan for the future to address her mistakes. She doesn't feel like she is a bad person for making mistakes, but instead realizes that her processes of learning didn't work out and can be changed.

The STEM Road Map curriculum modules are designed for students from all backgrounds to be successful. Teachers can support meaningful learning in each module by encouraging beneficial SRL processes like those adopted by Miranda and illuminating and redirecting poor SRL processes like those adopted by Josie. Not only will encouraging productive SRL skills help students learn more STEM content in the modules (Peters, 2012), but it will also give students the ability to be life-long learners since they will build the skills to learn independently. The remainder of this chapter explains how SRL theory is embedded within the five sections of each module and points out ways to support students as they become independent learners of STEM.

BEFORE LEARNING – SETTING THE STAGE

The processes that are important to understand before attempting a learning task, such as the STEM Road Map curriculum modules, are the students' level of comfort with accomplishing the learning and what students already know about the topic. When

students are comfortable with attempting a learning task, they tend to take more risks in learning and as a result have deeper learning (Bandura, 1986). Several factors contribute to students' comfort for a learning task:

- They have accomplished a similar learning task.

- They have watched someone they can relate to accomplish a similar learning task.

- Other people encourage them to perform a task.

- The learner is excited about the learning task.

(Bandura, 1997)

The STEM Road Map curriculum modules are designed to foster excitement from the very beginning. Each module has an Introductory Activity/Engagement section that introduces the overall topic from a unique and exciting perspective, engaging the students to learn more in order to be able to accomplish the challenge. The Introductory Activity also has a design component that helps teachers assess what students already know about the topic of the module. In addition to the deliberate designs in the lesson plans to support SRL, teachers can support a high level of comfort with the learning challenge by finding out from students if they have accomplished the same kind of task and asking students to share what worked well for them. Additionally, teachers can be encouraging about student attempts toward solving the problem, but should be careful to give specific reasons why and not just generally say, for example, "You guys are smart." Specific feedback throughout the module will help students gauge the accuracy of the steps they take toward the final challenge.

DURING THE LEARNING – STAYING THE COURSE

Some students fear inquiry learning because they aren't sure what to do to be successful (Peters, 2010). However, the STEM Road Map curriculum modules are embedded with tools to help students pay attention to knowledge and skills that are important for the learning task and check their understanding along the way. One of the most important processes for learning is the ability for the learner to monitor their own progress while performing a learning task (Peters, 2012). The modules provide tools such as checklists and graphic organizers so that students can record what they know and can do and check whether they have a complete set of knowledge and skills. Teachers can support student self-monitoring by assessing these checklists and graphic organizers and either assuring students they are on the right track or encouraging them to learn a certain piece of knowledge or skill.

Another important process is that students pay attention to the correct concepts and skills during the STEM Road Map curriculum module. It is well known that novice

learners can have difficulty knowing what to pay attention to and tend to treat each possible avenue for information as equal (Benner, 1984). Experts, however, have a short list of ways to solve a particular problem and can get right to the most critical information or processes. Teachers are the experts in a classroom, and can illuminate for students (novice learners) ways to approach learning during the Activity/Investigation, Explanation, and Extension/Application portions of the lesson plans. For example, if a student is to research key features of roller coasters (height, speed, circular motion), and the student has a long list of where the roller coasters are located, teachers can step in and explain why they need to redirect their efforts. Students can then adopt the processes of the experts and become more skillful.

AFTER LEARNING – KNOWING WHAT WORKS

The classroom is a busy place, and it is often the case that there is no time for self-reflection on learning. Although skipping this reflective process may save time in the short term, it reduces the ability to take into account things that worked well, things that didn't, and ways to improve next time. In the long run, these skills are critical for students to become independent learners who can adapt to new situations. By investing in the time it takes to teach students SRL skills, teachers can save time later since students are finding ways that they can successfully learn and will be able to apply them to new situations. In the Assessment portion of the STEM Road Map curriculum modules as well as in the formative assessments throughout the modules, two processes in the after-learning phase are supported: (a) evaluating one's own performance, and (b) accounting for ways to adapt tactics that didn't work well. Students have many opportunities to self-assess in formative assessments, both in groups and individually, using the rubrics provided in the modules.

The designs of NGSS and Common Core Standards allow for students to learn in diverse ways, and the STEM Road Map curriculum modules emphasize that students can use a variety of tactics to complete the learning products. For example, students can use STEM Research Notebooks to record what they have learned during the various research activities. Notebook entries might include putting objectives in students' own words, compiling their prior learning on the topic, documenting new learning, providing proof of what they learned, and reflecting on what they felt successful doing and what they felt they still needed to work on. Perhaps a student didn't realize that they were supposed to connect what they already knew about concrete (that it was made of smaller pebbles cemented together) with what they learned about concrete (that it is a very complex substance that has only just been identified chemically). They could record this and in the next learning task would be prepared to begin connecting prior learning to new learning. Table 3.1 illustrates some of the activities in the Creating Global Bonds module and how they align to the SRL learning processes before, during, and after learning occurs.

Table 3.1. SRL Learning Process Components

Learning Process Components	Example from Creating Global Bonds Module	Lesson Number
Before Learning		
Motivates students	In the opening activity, small groups of students (2–3 per group) are presented with two to three images from a website (http://climate.nasa.gov/images-of-change#574-lake-mead-at-record-low). In their groups, they are to discern the general climate of the areas depicted in the images and discuss how climate change has potentially impacted these areas. Teachers may use a graphic organizer to support student inference-making.	Lesson 1
Evokes prior learning	Following that activity, distribute the map of global energy consumption found at (https://ourworldindata.org/energy-production-consumption). Allow students to make connections between energy use and climate change using another graphic organizer to help students make appropriate connections between the sources.	Lesson 1
During Learning		
Focuses on important features	After the first (synchronous or asynchronous) meeting with international partners, students should begin to compare data for areas of overlap and differences with respect to energy consumption and climate change.	Lesson 2
Helps students monitor their progress	Students in local and international groups compare data between both groups of students and look to align topics for further study. Data might be compared about specific energy use from today and future projections.	Lesson 2
After Learning		
Evaluates learning	Students write a white paper and present their ideas for solutions for excessive energy consumption, backing up their ideas with data.	Lesson 3
Takes account of what worked and what did not work	Students research other relevant audiences outside of their school and evaluate what these audiences would gain from their work.	Lesson 3

There are certain strategies or tactics that learners use for all phases of learning, although some of them are more productive than others. The STEM Road Map curriculum modules are designed to help students to use positive, high-impact strategies before, during, and after learning by:

1. evoking student prior understandings and motivational beliefs toward learning the topic;

2. pointing out the key knowledge and skills for the module and monitoring their performance; and

3. providing opportunities for students to self-reflect on the processes they use to learn and produce the challenge product.

Teachers who can use the learning theory behind the STEM Road Map curriculum modules to identify teachable moments can help students to develop strategies and tactics for learning that result in independent, motivated, and self-sustaining learners.

REFERENCES

Ausubel, D. P. (1963). *The psychology of meaningful verbal learning.* Grune & Stratton.

Bandura, A. (1986). *Social foundations of thought and action: A social cognitive theory.* Prentice-Hall, Inc.

Bandura, A. (1997). *Self-efficacy: The exercise of control.* Freeman.

Bembenutty, H., Cleary, T., & Kitsantas, A., (2013). *Self-regulated learning applied across diverse disciplines: A tribute to Barry J. Zimmerman.* Information Age Publishing.

Benner, P. (1984). *From novice to expert: Excellence and power in clinical nursing practice.* Addison-Wesley Publishing Company.

Cheema, J., & Kitsantas, A. (2013). Influences of disciplinary classroom climate on high school student self-efficacy and mathematics achievement: A look at gender and racial-ethnic differences. *International Journal of Science and Mathematics Education*, advance online publication. https://doi.org/10.1007/s10763-013-9454-4

Geary, D. C. (1995). Reflections of evolution and culture in children's cognition: Implications for mathematical development and instruction. *American Psychologist, 50*, 24–37.

Harold, R. D., Colarossi, L. G., & Mercier, L. R. (2007). *Smooth sailing or stormy waters? Family transitions through adolescence and their implications for practice and policy.* Erlbaum.

Hogan, K. (2000). Exploring a process view of students' knowledge about the nature of science. *Science Education, 84*, 51–70.

Lemke, J. L. (1997). Cognition, context and learning: A social semiotic process. In D. Kirshner & J. A. Whitson (Eds.), *Situated cognition: Social, semiotic, and psychological perspectives* (pp. 37–55). Erlbaum.

Peters, E. E. (2010). Shifting to a student-centered science classroom: An exploration of teacher and student changes in perceptions and practices. *Journal of Science Teacher Education*, 21(3), 329–349. https://doi.org/10.1007/s10972-009-9178-z

Peters, E. E. (2012). Developing content knowledge in students through explicit teaching of the nature of science: Influences of goal setting and self-monitoring. *Science & Education*, 21(6), 881–898. https://doi.org/10.1007/s11191-009-9219-1

Peters, E. E., & Kitsantas, A. (2010). The effect of nature of science metacognitive prompts on science students' content and nature of science knowledge, metacognition, and self-regulatory efficacy. *School Science and Mathematics*, 110, 382–396. https://doi.org/10.1111/j.1949-8594.2010.00050.x

Zimmerman, B. J. (2000). Attaining self-regulation: A social-cognitive perspective. In M. Boekaerts, P. Pintrich, & M. Zeidner (Eds.), *Handbook of self-regulation* (pp. 13–39). Academic Press.

Zimmerman, B., & Kitsantas, A. (2002). Acquiring writing revision and self-regulatory skill through observation and emulation. *Journal of Educational Psychology*, 94(4), 660–668.

STEM ROAD MAP CURRICULUM MODULE OVERVIEW

Anthony Pellegrino, Jennifer Drake-Patrick, Brad Rankin, Erin E. Peters-Burton, Janet B. Walton, and Carla C. Johnson

THEME: Sustainable Systems

LEAD DISCIPLINES: Science/Social Studies

MODULE SUMMARY

Energy consumption and climate change are related and pressing issues for all humanity. Scientific research and media reports provide a tremendous amount of information related to these issues. Efforts to bring this information into classrooms are challenging because of the complexity and global scale of the issues. Drawing connections between energy consumption and climate change in students' own communities and then extending these connections on a global scale will minimize this challenge and enhance students' awareness of their roles as global citizens. The intention of this module is to help students explore energy consumption and climate change in their own communities and connect that information with communities around the world through an international blog. The data gathered and connections made with international partners will allow students to seek practical, measurable, and impactful means to address issues of energy consumption and climate change locally and globally. The global bonds created through this module will help students see the interrelatedness of global environments and how knowledge of local energy issues and international collaboration can raise awareness of issues of energy consumption and climate change (adapted from Peters-Burton et al., 2015; see www.routledge.com/products/9781138804234).

ESTABLISHED GOALS/OBJECTIVES

The goal for this module is for students to create an action plan to address issues of energy consumption and climate change. Students will gather data on energy consumption and climate change in their communities and regions and share that information with international student partners undertaking similar tasks. Together, students will function as international partners and undergo problem-solving activities to examine issues that are both common across and unique to each community. International teams, arranged through electronic platforms that allow teachers to coordinate with international colleagues with whom they can communicate, will then create blog posts in which they make visible their efforts to address issues in ways that are both local and global in scope. Student partners will ultimately be expected to develop a white paper and interactive web-based presentation on local and international issues of energy consumption and climate change and ways their international connections informed how they examined and addressed the issues.

By the end of the module students will be able to:

a. Identify modes and trends in energy consumption in their communities and regions

b. Analyze how those patterns of energy consumption impact climate change

c. Partner with students internationally to coordinate efforts to synthesize energy consumption data and discern connections across contexts

d. Design and present an action plan to address issues of energy consumption and climate change

One of the crosscutting concepts in the project is patterns related to energy consumption and climate change. Throughout the project students will learn about local and regional energy use patterns and ways these might contribute to climate change. Beyond the critical local knowledge students will gain, the international connections will allow students to make connections between their community and the world through exploration of energy consumption and climate change. Students will engage in science and engineering practices such as developing and using models, planning and carrying out investigations, analyzing and interpreting data, using mathematics and computational thinking, constructing explanations (for science), and designing solutions (for engineering). Language arts objectives include engaging in arguments based upon evidence; obtaining, evaluating, and communicating information with international partners; and writing and presenting an action plan that includes ways the communities involved might address issues of energy consumption and climate change.

CHALLENGE AND/OR PROBLEM FOR STUDENTS TO SOLVE

Students are challenged to gather data related to energy consumption and the impact of climate change in their communities. Students will analyze these data for themes and connections and evaluate measures to mitigate climate change. In addition to the local focus for data collection, students will also be challenged to coordinate their efforts with those of students internationally. Forming international teams, students will look across contexts for trends in data and mitigating solutions to climate change. This work will be presented in a blog set up by the partners. Together, these partners will collaborate to identify commonalities and differences found in their respective research to develop an action plan. This action plan will be the conclusion of a white paper and interactive presentation shared with participating school groups as well as via the blog set up to document the work.

Driving Questions: How do issues of energy consumption and climate develop locally and internationally? Are there similarities and differences in energy consumption from local to international? How can international teams of students use local data collection to develop mitigating strategies to address climate change problems across contexts?

CONTENT STANDARDS ADDRESSED IN STEM ROAD MAP MODULE

Table 4.1. Next Generation Science Standards (NGSS)

Performance Objectives	Disciplinary Core Ideas and Crosscutting Concepts	Science and Engineering Practices
HS-ESS3-3 Create a computational simulation to illustrate the relationships among management of natural resources, the sustainability of human populations, and biodiversity. HS-ESS2-4 Use a model to describe how variations in the flow of energy into and out of Earth's systems result in changes in climate. HS-ESS3-5 Analyze geoscience data and the results from global climate models to make an evidence-based forecast of the current rate of global or regional climate change and associated future impacts to Earth systems.	*DISCIPLINARY CORE IDEAS* **ESS2.D: WEATHER AND CLIMATE** • Changes in the atmosphere due to human activity have increased carbon dioxide concentrations and thus affect climate. (HS-ESS2-6; HS-ESS2-4) • Current models predict that, although future regional climate changes will be complex and varied, average global temperatures will continue to rise. The outcomes predicted by global climate models strongly depend on the amounts of human-generated greenhouse gases added to the atmosphere each year and by the ways in which these gases are absorbed by the ocean and biosphere. (secondary to HS-ESS3-6) **ESS3.A: NATURAL RESOURCES** • Resource availability has guided the development of human society. (HS-ESS3-1) • All forms of energy production and other resource extraction have associated economic, social, environmental, and geopolitical costs and risks as well as benefits. New technologies and social regulations can change the balance of these factors. (HS-ESS3-2) **ESS3.C: HUMAN IMPACTS ON EARTH SYSTEMS** • The sustainability of human societies and the biodiversity that supports them requires responsible management of natural resources. (HS-ESS3-3) • Scientists and engineers can make major contributions by developing technologies that produce less pollution and waste and that preclude ecosystem degradation. (HS-ESS3-4) **ESS3.D: GLOBAL CLIMATE CHANGE** • Though the magnitudes of human impacts are greater than they have ever been, so too are human abilities to model, predict, and manage current and future impacts. (HS-ESS3-5)	*Analyzing and Interpreting Data* • Analyze data using computational models in order to make valid and reliable scientific claims. (HS-ESS3-5) *Using Mathematics and Computational Thinking* • Create a computational model or simulation of a phenomenon, designed device, process, or system. (HS-ESS3-3) • Use a computational representation of phenomena or design solutions to describe and/or support claims and/or explanations. (HS-ESS3-6) *Constructing Explanations and Designing Solutions* • Construct an explanation based on valid and reliable evidence obtained from a variety of sources (including students' own investigations, models, theories, simulations, peer review) and the assumption that theories and laws that describe the natural world operate today as they did in the past and will continue to do so in the future. (HS-ESS3-1)

HS-ESS3-6 Use a computational representation to illustrate the relationships among Earth systems and how those relationships are being modified due to human activity.	• Through computer simulations and other studies, important discoveries are still being made about how the ocean, the atmosphere, and the biosphere interact and are modified in response to human activities. (HS-ESS3-6) **ETS1.B: DEVELOPING POSSIBLE SOLUTIONS** • When evaluating solutions, it is important to take into account a range of constraints, including cost, safety, reliability, and aesthetics, and to consider social, cultural, and environmental impacts. (secondary to HS-ESS3-2; secondary HS-ESS3-4) *CROSSCUTTING CONCEPTS* **STABILITY AND CHANGE** Change and rates of change can be quantified and modeled over very short or very long periods of time. Some system changes are irreversible. **CAUSE AND EFFECT** Empirical evidence is required to differentiate between cause and correlation and make claims about specific causes and effects. **SYSTEMS AND SYSTEM MODELS** When investigating or describing a system, the boundaries and initial conditions of the system need to be defined and their inputs and outputs analyzed and described using models. **CONNECTIONS TO ENGINEERING, TECHNOLOGY, AND APPLICATIONS OF SCIENCE** Influence of Science, Engineering, and Technology on Society and the Natural World Modern civilization depends on major technological systems. New technologies can have deep impacts on society and the environment, including some that were not anticipated. - **CONNECTIONS TO NATURE OF SCIENCE** Science is a Human Endeavor Science is a result of human endeavors, imagination, and creativity.	• Design or refine a solution to a complex real-world problem, based on scientific knowledge, student-generated sources of evidence, prioritized criteria, and tradeoff considerations. (HS-ESS3-4) *Engaging in Argument from Evidence* • Evaluate competing design solutions to a real-world problem based on scientific ideas and principles, empirical evidence, and logical arguments regarding relevant factors (e.g., economic, societal, environmental, ethical considerations). (HS-ESS3-2)

Table 4.2. Common Core Mathematics and English Language Arts (ELA) Standards

Common Core Mathematics Standards	Common Core English Language Arts (ELA) Standards
MATHEMATICS PRACTICES MP1 Make sense of problems and persevere in solving them. MP3 Construct viable arguments and critique the reasoning of others. MP8 Look for and express regularity in repeated reasoning. *MATHEMATICS CONTENT* CCSSMath.Content.HSA-REI.B.3 Solve linear equations and inequalities in one variable, including equations with coefficients represented by letters. CCSS.Math.Content.HSA-REI.A.2 Solve simple rational and radical equations in one variable, and give examples showing how extraneous solutions may arise.	*READING STANDARDS* RH 11-12.1 Cite specific textual evidence to support analysis of primary and secondary sources, connecting insights gained from specific details to an understanding of the text as a whole. RH 11-12.2 Determine the central ideas or information of a primary or secondary source; provide an accurate summary that makes clear the relationships among the key details and ideas. RH.11-12.3 Evaluate various explanations for actions or events and determine which explanation best accords with textual evidence, acknowledging where the text leaves matters uncertain RH 11-12.7 Integrate and evaluate multiple sources of information presented in diverse formats and media (e.g., visually, quantitatively, as well as in words) in order to address a question or solve a problem.

NATIONAL SCIENCE TEACHING ASSOCIATION

Table 4.3. 21st Century Skills Addressed in STEM Road Map Module

21st Century Skills	Learning Skills & Technology Tools (from P21 framework)	Teaching Strategies	Evidence of Success
21st century interdisciplinary themes	Global Awareness Civic Literacy Environmental Literacy	Teachers will direct student attention towards connections between energy consumption and climate change and how efforts to mitigate climate change can be addressed locally and through international partnerships.	Students will develop a robust understanding of energy consumption in their local communities and identify ways in which climate change has and is expected to affect their communities. Students will also explore ways that energy consumption and climate change impacts global environments and seek ways that may help to curb climate change at home and abroad.
Learning and innovation skills	Creativity & Innovation Critical Thinking & Problem Solving Communication & Collaboration	Teachers will offer access to resources related to energy consumption and climate change to help students understand the role local and international communities play in addressing these issues. Additionally, teachers will guide students in problem-solving strategies to support the work of groups to identify challenges and develop means to address these challenges.	Students will work to find and collaborate with international partners to develop a blog dedicated to environmental issues of energy and climate change. Through this blog, student groups will share findings of their work to identify themes related to energy consumption and climate change. This effort will also include work to communicate connections and themes through the blog and document ways groups elect to put forth ways to mitigate climate change in their communities and in the communities of their partners.
Information, media and technology skills	Information Literacy Media Literacy ICT Literacy	Teachers will require the use of different reliable resources for this project and challenge students to share their work on a blog they develop and maintain.	Students will use a variety of reliable resources and cite these resources accordingly in their final products, which will be shared in part through a blog developed and maintained by the student groups.
Life and career skills	Flexibility & Adaptability Initiative & Self-Direction Social & Cross Cultural Skills Productivity & Accountability Leadership & Responsibility	Teachers will provide checkpoints for students to self-monitor their progress at each of the phases of the project.	Students will articulate their goals for each checkpoint for the project and devise strategic plans to show progress toward their goals. Students will work effectively in collaborative groups and be clear about roles of each member.

Table 4.4. English Language Development Standards Addressed in STEM Road Map Module

English Language Development Standards: Grades 9–12 (WIDA, 2012)

ELD Standard 1: Social and Instructional Language
   English language learners communicate for Social and Instructional purposes within the school setting.
ELD Standard 2: The Language of Language Arts
   English language learners communicate information, ideas and concepts necessary for academic success in the content area of Language Arts.
ELD Standard 3: The Language of Mathematics
   English language learners communicate information, ideas and concepts necessary for academic success in the content area of Mathematics
ELD Standard 4: The Language of Science.
   English language learners communicate information, ideas and concepts necessary for academic success in the content area of Science
ELD Standard 5: The Language of Social Studies
   English language learners communicate information, ideas and concepts necessary for academic success in the content area of Social Studies.

STEM RESEARCH NOTEBOOK

Each student will maintain a STEM Research Notebook that will serve as a place for students to organize their work throughout the module. All written work in the module should be included in the notebook, including records of students' thoughts and ideas, fictional accounts based on the concepts in the module, and records of student progress through the Engineering Design Process. The notebooks may be maintained across subject areas, giving students the opportunity to see that although their classes may be separated during the school day the knowledge they gain is connected.

A three-ring binder works well for the Research Notebooks since students will include a variety of handouts in the Research Notebook. You may wish to have students create divided sections in order to easily access work from various disciplines during the module. Students will have the opportunity to create a cover and table of contents for their Research Notebooks (see Lesson 1 Activity/Investigation, ELA). You may also wish to have students include the STEM Research Notebook Guidelines provided below in their notebooks.

Emphasize to students that scientists and other researchers maintain detailed Research Notebooks in their work. These notebooks are crucial to researchers' work since they contain critical information and track the researchers' progress. These notebooks are often considered legal documents for scientists who are pursuing patents or who wish to provide evidence of their discovery process. Introduce to students the importance of organizing all information in a Research Notebook.

STUDENT HANDOUT

STEM RESEARCH NOTEBOOK GUIDELINES

A critical part of being a STEM professional is to capture your ideas, inventions, experimentation, questions, observations, and other work details in a notebook so that it can be used as a tool to continue your thinking about projects and problems that you encounter in class and in the real world. It is important to take careful notes and include lots of detail for use in the future. Don't forget the purpose of the STEM Research Notebook is for your personal work. Feel free to include things not on the list below – whatever helps your learning move forward should be included.

For this module, "Creating Global Connections," you will be using your STEM Research Notebook as a primary tool to track your thoughts, ideas, questions, and connect your daily work back to the big problem or challenge you are working to solve.

There are several important things that you will keep in your STEM Research Notebook. It is important that you organize your daily entries using the following headings:

1. CHAPTER TOPIC/TITLE OF PROBLEM/CHALLENGE – You will start a new "chapter" in your STEM Research Notebook with each new module. This is the topic/title of the big problem or challenge that your team is working to solve in the current module. This will be presented during the first lesson of the module – so you will only record it in the beginning and as helpful as you progress through the module.

2. DAILY – Each day you will start at the top of a new page and enter the DATE and TOPIC OF LESSON ACTIVITY FOR THE DAY. This is how you will begin your daily entry. Enter the page number for this entry on the page and also in the Table of Contents.

3. DAILY – INFORMATION GATHERED FROM BACKGROUND RESEARCH – This would include information from outside resources (i.e., citations, interviews, note taking).

4. DAILY – INFORMATION GAINED FROM CLASS OR DISCUSSIONS WITH TEAM MEMBERS – This includes any notes and/or drawings that you will take in your class that will enable you to build your knowledge needed to solve your big problem/challenge.

5. DAILY – NEW DATA COLLECTED FROM INVESTIGATIONS – This would include qualitative and quantitative data gathered from experiments and/or investigations/activities in class.

6. DAILY – ARCHIVAL DOCUMENTS – This includes handouts and other resources that you may receive/collect in class that will help you solve your big problem/challenge. Paste or staple these documents directly into your STEM Research Notebook for safe keeping and easy access later.

7. DAILY – PERSONAL REFLECTIONS – This is where you will record your own personal reflections on what you are learning and/or thinking.

8. LESSON PROMPTS – This is the question or statement that your teacher assigns to you within each lesson focused on applying what you learned to help you solve your big problem/challenge. You will respond to the prompt.

9. OTHER ITEMS – This would be other items your teacher may assign or other ideas/questions you may have.

MODULE LAUNCH

In the opening activity, small groups of students (two to three per group) are presented with two to three images from a website (http://climate.nasa.gov/images-of-change#574-lake-mead-at-record-low). In their groups, they are to discern the general climate of the areas depicted in the images and discuss how climate change has potentially impacted these areas. Teachers may use a graphic organizer to support student inference-making. Following that activity, distribute the map of global energy consumption found at (https://ourworldindata.org/worlds-energy-problem). Allow students to make connections between energy use and climate change using another graphic organizer to help them make appropriate connections between the sources. In addition, the International Energy Agency offers an annual energy statistics document for those teachers who might like to get students to explore energy consumption and production statistics in more detail. The 2021 report can be found at (www.iea.org/reports/electricity-information-overview)

PREREQUISITE KEY KNOWLEDGE

Upper-level high school students have had some experience with environmental science in middle or high school, so they should have some basic knowledge about the difference between climate and weather, energy use and production, and the ways in which humans have impacted the environment. Foundational knowledge around these ideas will be important for successful implementation of the project. Additionally, students will ideally have some working knowledge of technology and ways to create using technology. Some statistical knowledge about calculating means and standard deviations will be needed for analysis of the International Energy Agency report.

Table 4.5. Prerequisite Key Knowledge and Sample Differentiation Strategies

Prerequisite Key Knowledge	Application of Knowledge	Differentiation for Students Needing Knowledge
Climate versus weather	Students will be examining current climate conditions in their communities.	Students needing support for this knowledge can visit the Colorado State University produced video (www.youtube.com/watch?v=VHgyUa7UQ7Y), which offers a clear and visually compelling presentation of these two phenomena.
Energy use and production	Students will be gathering and synthesizing data related to energy use in their communities.	Students who need support to better understand energy use and production could look to the International Energy Agency's annual report (www.iea.org/reports/electricity-information-overview). In this report, students will find a variety of easy-to-read data tables that show energy use by nation, region, and longitudinally.
Human impact on the environment	Students will be looking across data related to climate changes and energy use to discern patterns related to human impact on the environment.	Students who need support to gather and analyze data will have the support of peers and the teacher. Teachers should be mindful of student pairing to support all students' learning. Assigning roles to partners and establishing periodic member and teacher checks for understanding and progress may be a valuable strategy. There are many useful websites about data gathering and analysis at the middle school and high school level such as http://stattrek.com and Khan Academy.
Hypothesis development	Students will review activating images on day 1 and develop a hypothesis of the relationship between energy consumption and climate change.	Student partners may need additional support to guide them through hypothesis development. There are many useful websites about statistics at the middle school and high school level to help with null and alternative hypotheses such as http://stattrek.com/ and Khan Academy.

POTENTIAL STEM MISCONCEPTIONS

The following commonly held misconceptions are provided as a sample so that you can be alert to student misunderstanding of the science concepts presented and used during this module. The American Association for the Advancement of Science (AAAS) has also identified misconceptions that students frequently hold regarding science concepts. This information, in addition to other information about misconceptions, can be accessed at www.nsta.org/blog/do-you-know-what-you-do-not-know.

Teachers should fundamentally know differences between weather and climate and the ways these ideas are sometimes conflated in media coverage related to climate change. NASA offers a useful introduction to these terms: (www.nasa.gov/mission_pages/noaa-n/climate/climate_weather.html). Teachers should also have an understanding of the scientific community's scholarship on climate change at a basic level and the arguments of those who disagree with the broad scientific community.

In terms of lesson execution, teachers should be aware of digital media and the affordances these media have on student learning. Edutopia offers resources related to classroom technology: (www.edutopia.org/technology-integration-guide-resources). Grainne Conole and Martin Dyke (2004) published a paper over a decade ago that still offers an important description of affordances and technology: (www.tandfonline.com/doi/full/10.1080/0968776042000216183). It may be useful for teachers to review for background information.

Table 4.6. Sample STEM Misconceptions

Topic	Student Misconception	Explanation
Climate: Prevailing conditions such as temperature, air pressure, humidity, precipitation, sunshine, cloudiness, and winds in an area averaged over years. Climate is the statistical analysis of weather.	Climate is simply long-term weather and therefore can't be predicted.	There are significant differences between weather and climate processes and how they are studied and forecast. Weather is the atmospheric conditions at any given time or place. Climate is understood as the atmospheric conditions averaged over a long period of time and over a large area.
Global warming: Global warming is caused by increased greenhouse gases in the atmosphere. These gases include carbon dioxide and water vapor, which trap infrared radiation from the warmed surface of the Earth.	Global warming is caused by the ozone hole because the hole lets in more radiation. (Ozone hole created by chemicals like hair spray.)	The ozone layer protects the planet from the sun's harmful radiation. A depletion of ozone allows more UV light to reach the surface, but is not an important factor leading to increased temperature on Earth. Banning CFCs from spray cans has caused the ozone hole to stop growing.
Climate change: Small changes in the atmosphere's composition or temperature can have a large effect.	The atmosphere is large and small amounts of carbon dioxide or a few degrees of temperature change can't make much difference.	An important source of evidence for climate change comes from observations that *average* weather has changed for a region.
Differences between weather and climate: Weather involves phenomena that last a short period of time. Climate can be thought of as the average weather for a region. There is a link between climate change and weather, but any particular weather "event" cannot "prove" that climate change is happening.	Weather anomalies can be used as evidence for or against climate change.	An important source of evidence for climate change comes from observations that *average* weather has changed for a region.

SAMPLE STRATEGIES FOR DIFFERENTIATING INSTRUCTION WITHIN THIS MODULE

For the purposes of this curriculum module, differentiated instruction is conceptualized as a way to tailor instruction (including process, content, and product) to various student needs in your class. A number of differentiation strategies are integrated into lessons across the module. The problem and/or project-based learning (PBL) approach used in the lessons is designed to address students' multiple intelligences by providing a variety of entry points and methods to investigate the key concepts in the module (for example, investigating the production and consumption of electricity at local, regional, and global levels). Differentiation strategies for students needing support in prerequisite knowledge can be found in the Prerequisite Key Knowledge section. You are encouraged to use information gained about student prior knowledge during introductory activities and discussions to inform your instructional differentiation. Strategies incorporated into this lesson include:

Flexible Grouping: Students work collaboratively in a variety of activities throughout this module. Grouping strategies you may choose to employ include student-led grouping, placing students in groups according to ability level, grouping students randomly, or grouping them so that students in each group have complementary strengths (for instance, one student might be strong in mathematics, another in art, and another in writing). Beginning in Lesson 2, you may wish to maintain the student groupings from Lesson 1 or regroup students according to one of the strategies described here. You may therefore wish to consider grouping students in Lesson 2 into design teams that they will maintain throughout the remainder of the module.

Various Environmental Learning Contexts: Students have the opportunity to learn in various contexts throughout the module, including alone, in groups, in quiet reading and research-oriented activities, and in active learning in inquiry and design activities. In addition, students learn in a variety of ways, including inquiry activities, journaling, reading fiction and non-fiction texts, watching videos, class discussion, and conducting web-based research.

Assessments: Students are assessed in a variety of ways throughout the module, including individual and collaborative formative and summative assessments. Students have the opportunity to produce work via written text, oral presentations, media presentations, and modeling. You may choose to provide students with additional choices of media for their products (for example PowerPoint presentations, posters, or student-created websites or blogs).

Other strategies you may choose to employ include:

Compacting: Based upon student prior knowledge you may wish to adjust instructional activities for students who exhibit prior mastery of a learning objective. For instance, if some students exhibit mastery of comparison of two variables in mathematics in Lesson 1, you may wish to limit the amount of time they spend practicing these skills and instead introduce ELA or social studies connections with associated activities.

Tiered Assignments & Scaffolding: Based upon your understanding of student ability, you may wish to provide students with variations on activities by adding complexity to assignments and/or providing more or fewer learning supports for activities throughout the module based upon student understanding of concepts and mastery of skills. For instance, some students may need additional support in identifying key search words and phrases for web-based research or may benefit from cloze sentence handouts to enhance vocabulary understanding. Other students may benefit from expanded reading selections and additional reflective writing. Others may benefit from working with manipulatives and other visual representations of mathematical concepts. You may also wish to work with your school librarian to compile a set of topical resources at a variety of reading levels.

Strategies for English Language Learners (ELLs): Students who are developing proficiency in English language skills require additional supports to simultaneously learn academic content and the specialized language associated with specific content areas. WIDA has created a framework for providing support to these students and provides rubrics and guidance on differentiating instructional materials for ELLs, providing five overarching learning standards (see https://wida.wisc.edu/teach/standards/eld). In particular, ELL students may benefit from additional sensory supports, including images, physical modeling, and graphic representations of module content as well as interactive support through collaborative work. This module incorporates a variety of sensory supports and provides ongoing opportunities for ELL students to work collaboratively. The focus in this module is on various ways to examine energy consumption and production in a global context and provides opportunities to access the culturally diverse experiences of ELL students in the classroom.

Teachers differentiating instruction for ELL students should carefully consider the needs of these students as they introduce and use academic language in various language domains (listening, speaking, reading, and writing) throughout this module. In order to adequately differentiate instruction for ELL students, teachers should have an understanding of the proficiency level of each student. WIDA provides an

assessment tool to assist teachers in assessing English language proficiency levels at https://wida.wisc.edu/assess/access/tests. The following 9–12 WIDA standards are relevant to this module:

> Standard 1: Social and Instructional Language. Focus on social behavior in group work and class discussions.

> Standard 2: The language of Language Arts. Focus on forms of print, elements of text, picture books, comprehension strategies, main ideas/details, persuasive language, creating informational text, and editing and revising.

> Standard 3: The language of Mathematics. Focus on numbers and operations, patterns, number sense, measurement, and strategies for problem solving.

> Standard 4: The language of Science. Focus on safety practices, magnetism, energy sources, scientific process, and scientific inquiry.

> Standard 5: The language of Social Studies. Focus on change from past to present, historical events, resources, transportation, map reading, and location of objects and places.

SAFETY CONSIDERATIONS FOR SCIENCE ACTIVITIES

Student safety is a primary consideration in all subjects but is an area of particular concern in science where students may interact with tools and materials with which they are unfamiliar and which may pose additional safety risks. You should ensure that your classroom setup is in accord with your school's safety policies and that students are familiar with basic safety procedures, including wearing protective equipment (safety glasses, gloves, etc.) in laboratory settings, and are familiar with the location of protective equipment and emergency exit procedures. The Council of State Science Supervisors (CSSS) provides information about classroom science safety including a safety checklist for science classrooms. See the NSTA website at www.nsta.org/topics/safety to access this information and for links to other science safety related resources.

Teachers should develop an internet/blog protocol with students if guidelines are not already in place. Since students will use the internet to acquire the needed data for their research, teachers should monitor students' access to the internet to ensure that students are only accessing websites that are clearly identified by the teacher. Further, the teacher should inform parents/guardians that students will create online multimedia presentations of their research and that these projects will be closely monitored by the teacher. It is recommended that the teacher not allow any website posts created by students to "go public" without being approved by the teacher.

DESIRED OUTCOMES AND MONITORING SUCCESS

Table 4.7. Desired Outcomes and Evidence of Success

Desired Outcome	Evidence of Success in Achieving Identified Outcome	
Students will recognize the similarities and differences of energy consumption and climate change across local and international contexts, and be able to use those associated data to develop strategies and actions to effect change related to both topics.	Finding and analyzing energy consumption and climate change data.	a. Developing a partnership with international students to examine data across contexts, identify commonalities, and identify differences. b. Developing an action plan with international partners that includes strategies appropriate to affecting energy consumption and climate change.

ASSESSMENT PLAN

Table 4.8 provides an overview of the major group and individual products and deliverables that comprise the assessment for this module. See Chapter 5 for a full assessment map of formative and summative assessments in this module.

Table 4.8. Major Products/Deliverables in Lead Disciplines – Group and Individual

Lesson	Major Group Products/ Deliverables	Major Individual Products/ Deliverables
1	Data gathering and analysis artifact (Blog 1) White paper synthesizing research	• Community energy consumption and climate change data analysis • Contributions to group projects • Individual contributions to research for background knowledge • Individual contributions to analysis
2	Action plan and strategies to support energy efficiency and mitigation of climate change (Blog 2 & 3)	• Community energy consumption and climate change data analysis • Contributions to group projects • Individual contributions to research for background knowledge • Individual contributions to analysis
3	Presentation of findings and strategies	• Contributions to group projects • Individual contributions to research for background knowledge • Individual contributions to analysis

RESOURCES

Teachers have the option to co-teach portions of this unit and may want to combine classes for activities such as mathematical modeling, discussing global influences, or conducting research. The media specialist can help teachers locate resources for students to view and read about the production and consumption of energy and to provide technical help with spreadsheets, timeline software, and multimedia production software. Special educators and reading specialists can help find supplemental sources for students needing extra support in reading and writing.

School-based Individuals: Teachers can opt to co-teach portions of this module and may want to combine classes for activities such as establishing international partnerships, community mapping, and calculating energy usage. A media specialist can help teachers locate resources and establish the blog features.

Technology: Internet access, a blogging platform, and a means to communicate with international partners (e.g., epals, Zoom, Edmodo, globalclassroom, ilearn-USA).

Community: Local and resources such as energy companies are needed to provide local and regional energy consumption data.

Materials

Internet resources including blogging platform and international classroom project exchange platform (e.g., epals, Skype in the Classroom, Edmodo, globalclassroom, iEARN-USA).

Graphic organizers to support students making connections across topics (energy consumption and climate change) and making inferences.

International Partners: Teachers who are new to classroom projects done across schools might benefit from reading the brief article titled "Pen Pals in the 21st Century" (www.edutopia.org/blog/pen-pals-in-21st-century-lisa-mims).

In order to facilitate the international partnership required in this module, teachers will have to investigate the most appropriate means to connect with teachers at schools internationally far enough ahead of time to best align project goals with calendars. Sites such as epals, Skype in the Classroom, Edmodo, globalclassroom, and iEARN-USA invite teachers to propose projects with other teachers around the world and easily coordinate objectives, calendars, language differences, and so forth to facilitate an international school partnership. Likewise, for U.S.-based teachers, U.S. Department of Defense schools (found at www.dodea.edu) might serve as a potential international partnership. Prior to commencement of the project, the teacher(s) should have already made international connections (using resources such as epals, Skype in the Classroom, Edmodo, globalclassroom, iEARN-USA) to facilitate the launching of the project. Teachers should be flexible especially during days 1–5 to allow for partners to become established.

STEM ROAD MAP MODULE TIMELINE

Table 4.9. STEM Road Map Module Schedule Week One

Day 1	Day 2	Day 3	Day 4	Day 5
Lesson 1	*Lesson 1*	*Lesson 1*	*Lesson 1*	*Lesson 1*
Energy Consumption and Climate Change: At Home and Around the World	*Energy Consumption and Climate Change: At Home and Around the World*	*Energy Consumption and Climate Change: At Home and Around the World*	*Energy Consumption and Climate Change: At Home and Around the World*	*Energy Consumption and Climate Change: At Home and Around the World*
Students will examine images related to climate change. Students will also review energy consumption data to discern trends and themes. **Expected Daily Outcome:** Image analysis document	Students will develop introductory hypothesis about relationships between energy consumption and climate change. Students can navigate to the Intergovernmental Panel on Climate Change to agree upon the review process for data collection and dissemination. They can then view a variety of articles published by organizations that are skeptical of climate change science. The American Enterprise Institute is perhaps the most prominent of these organizations. **Expected Daily Outcome:** Hypothesis statement	Students will be paired to examine local and regional energy companies and government resources to find types of energy in their localities and energy consumption data. Partners will collect these data for their first blog entry **Expected Daily Outcome:** Data collection guide draft	Student pairs will continue to examine energy type and consumption data. Partners will collect these data for their first blog entry **Expected Daily Outcome:** Data collection guide final	Student pairs will identify international partners and work across contexts to review the project goal, collect the similar data about their respective communities, and agree on outputs (blogs, white paper, and presentation). Groups should also prepare their blog entry as an overview of the project to share with their international partners. **Expected Daily Outcome:** Blog 1 draft, partners' contact information

Table 4.10. STEM Road Map Module Schedule Week Two

Day 6	Day 7	Day 8	Day 9	Day 10
Lesson 1 *Energy Consumption and Climate Change: At Home and Around the World* International teams will work to refine goals of the project with international partners. International partners will come together (synchronously or asynchronously) to look for commonalities and differences across data related to energy consumption and climate change in their respective communities. **Expected Daily outcome:** Blog 1 final	*Lesson 2* *Making International Connections* Teams will engage in peer review of students' findings and blog postings with data from international settings. **Expected Daily Outcome:** Notes from all partners on local/regional data	*Lesson 2* *Making International Connections* From the themes that emerged in the first blog post, teams will identify the top 3 challenges they would like to address. **Expected Daily Outcome:** Themes related to energy consumption and climate change across contexts	*Lesson 2* *Making International Connections* Students will complete the problem-solving activity from Day 8 in which teams identify common problems. Today, they will focus on brainstorming solutions. **Expected Daily Outcome:** Problem-solving activity related to combined data	*Lesson 2* *Making International Connections* Students will identify possible solutions that are feasible for each local context and determine ways they might measure success of these mitigating solutions. **Expected Daily Outcome:** Problem-solving activity related to combined data

Table 4.11. STEM Road Map Module Schedule Week Three

Day 11	Day 12	Day 13	Day 14	Day 15
Lesson 2 *Making International Connections* Writing out ideas for Blog 2, which focuses on a synthesis of the similarities and differences in terms of energy consumption and issues related to climate change across contexts. **Expected Daily Outcome:** Blog 2 draft	*Lesson 2* *Making International Connections* Finalize draft of Blog 2 **Expected Daily Outcome:** Blog 2 final	*Lesson 3* *Using Data to Impact Energy Consumption and Climate Change* Days 13–17 involve developing a white paper, which synthesizes data and ideas from Blog 2 and combines it into a more formal document with specific recommendations based on data.	*Lesson 3* *Using Data to Impact Energy Consumption and Climate Change* Research day to look to traditional white paper formats. The USDA prepared a white paper on climate change that may be useful to discuss for formatting (search "Climate Change Science White Paper" from the USDA).	*Lesson 3* *Using Data to Impact Energy Consumption and Climate Change* Research day with beginnings of the paper taking shape. **Expected Daily Outcome:** White paper outline shared with all partners

Table 4.12. STEM Road Map Module Schedule Week Four

Day 16	Day 17	Day 18	Day 19	Day 20
Lesson 3	*Lesson 3*	*Lesson 3*	*Lesson 3*	*Lesson 3*
Using Data to Impact Energy Consumption and Climate Change	*Using Data to Impact Energy Consumption and Climate Change*	*Using Data to Impact Energy Consumption and Climate Change*	*Using Data to Impact Energy Consumption and Climate Change*	*Using Data to Impact Energy Consumption and Climate Change*
Peer review of the white paper draft.	Beginning of developing a presentation that includes international and local data and mitigating strategies to address the problem(s) teams agreed to address.	Continue presentation development and finalization of white paper	Continue presentation development.	Continue presentation development.
Expected Daily Outcome: White paper draft shared with all partners	**Expected Daily Outcomes:** White paper near final draft	**Expected Daily Outcomes:** White paper near final draft	**Expected Daily Outcome:** White paper final	**Expected Daily Outcomes:** Presentation draft and identification of at least two potential outlets for presentation
	Ideas shared with all partners about potential places to share data, findings, and recommendations (partners look to local and regional communities as well as international outlets)	Ideas shared with all partners about potential places to share data, findings, and recommendations (partners look to local and regional communities as well as international outlets)		

ASSESSMENT MAP FOR THE CREATING GLOBAL BONDS MODULE

Toni A. May, Erin E. Peters-Burton, and Carla C. Johnson

Starting in the middle years and continuing into secondary education, when the word *assessment* is mentioned one of the first things that traditionally comes to mind is "grades." These grades may take the form of a letter or a percentage, but they typically are used as a representation of a student's content mastery. Classroom assessment, however, if well thought out and implemented can offer stakeholders (teachers, parents, students) valuable information about student learning and misconceptions that does not necessarily come in the form of a grade (Popham, 2013).

The *STEM Road Map Curriculum Series* provides a set of assessments for each module that encourages teachers to use assessment information for more than assigning a grade to students. Instead, assessments such as student journaling in STEM Research Notebooks, collaborative presentations, constructing graphic organizers, and other activities requiring students to actively engage in their learning should be used to move student learning forward. While other curriculum series with assessments may include objective type (multiple-choice or matching) tests, quizzes, or worksheets, we have intentionally avoided these forms of assessments to better align assessment strategies with teacher instruction and student learning techniques. Since the focus of *Creating Global Bonds* is on project- or problem-based STEM curriculum and instruction which focuses on higher-level thinking skills, appropriate authentic and performance assessments were developed to elicit the most reliable and valid indication of student ability growth (Brookhart & Nitko, 2008).

COMPREHENSIVE ASSESSMENT SYSTEM

Assessment throughout all STEM Road Map curriculum modules acts as a system with both formative and summative working together to provide teachers with quality information on student learning. Formative assessment occurs when the teacher finds out formally or informally what a student knows for a smaller, defined concept

DOI: 10.4324/9781003362371-7

or skill and provides timely feedback to the student about their level of proficiency. Summative assessments occur when students have performed all activities in the module and are given a cumulative performance evaluation to demonstrate their growth in learning. A comprehensive assessment system can be thought of as a sporting event. Formative assessments are the practices; it is important to accomplish them consistently, they provide feedback to help students improve their learning, and making mistakes is worthwhile as long as students are given an opportunity to learn from them. Summative assessments are the competitions; students need to be prepared to perform at the best of their ability. Without multiple opportunities to practice skills along the way through formative assessments, students will not have the best chance of demonstrating growth in abilities through summative assessments (Black & Wiliam, 1998).

EMBEDDED FORMATIVE ASSESSMENTS IN CREATING GLOBAL BONDS

Formative assessments in this module serve two main purposes: (1) to provide feedback to students about their learning, and (2) to provide important information for the teacher to inform immediate instructional needs. Providing feedback to students is particularly important when conducting problem- or project-based learning because students take on much of the responsibility for learning, and teachers must facilitate student learning in an informed way. For example, if a student is required to conduct research for the Activity/Investigate phase and is not familiar with what constitutes a reliable resource, they may develop misconceptions based on poor information. When a teacher monitors this learning with formative assessments and provides students with specific feedback related to the instructional goals, students are less likely to develop incomplete or incorrect conceptions with their independent investigations. When teachers use formative assessment to detect a problem with student learning and act on this information, these teachable moments help to move student learning forward.

Formative assessments come in a variety of formats. They can be informal, such as asking students probing questions related to student knowledge or tasks, or as simple as observing students engaged in an activity to gather information about student skills. Formative assessments can also be formal, such as a written quiz or a laboratory practical. Regardless of the type, there are three key steps that must be completed when using formative assessments (Sondergeld et al., 2010). The assessment is first delivered to students for teachers to collect data. Next, teachers analyze the data (student responses) to determine student strengths and areas that need additional support. Finally, teachers use the results from information collected to modify lessons and

create learning environments that reinforce weak points in student learning. If student learning information is not used to modify instruction the assessment cannot be considered formative in nature.

Formative assessments can be about content, science process skills, or even learning skills. When a formative assessment focuses on content it assesses student knowledge about the Disciplinary Core Ideas from NGSS or content objectives from Common Core mathematics or English language arts. Content-focused formative assessments ask students questions about declarative knowledge regarding the concepts they have been learning. Process skills formative assessments examine the extent to which a student can perform science and engineering practices from the NGSS or process objectives from Common Core mathematics or English language arts, such as constructing an argument. Learning skills can also be assessed formatively by asking students to reflect on the ways they learn best during a module and identify ways they could have learned more. Chapter 3, "How Students Learn in Grades 9–12," addresses more of the learning processes that can be assessed formatively.

WHAT IS AN ASSESSMENT MAP?

Assessment maps or blueprints can be used to ensure alignment between classroom instruction and assessment. If what students are learning in the classroom is not the same as the content they are being assessed over, the resultant judgment made on student learning will be invalid (Brookhart & Nitko, 2008). Therefore, this issue of instruction and assessment alignment is critical. Table 5.1 lists all assessments in *Creating Global Bonds* by lesson, indicates if the assessment should be completed as a group or an individual, identifies the assessment as formative or summative in nature, and aligns the assessment with its corresponding learning objectives. Notice that there are far more formative assessments than summative assessments in the module. This is intentional to allow students to have multiple opportunities to practice their learning of new skills before completing a summative assessment. Note also that formative assessments are used to collect information on only one to two learning objectives at a time in order to focus potential relearning or instructional modifications on smaller and more manageable chunks of information. Conversely, summative assessments in the module cover many more learning objectives as they are traditionally used as final markers of student learning. This is not to say that information collected from summative assessments cannot or should not be used formatively. If teachers find that gaps in student learning continue to persist after a summative assessment is completed, it is important to revisit these existing misconceptions or content areas of weakness before moving on (Black et al., 2003).

ASSESSMENT MAP FOR CREATING GLOBAL BONDS MODULE

Table 5.1. Assessment Chart, Lead Disciplines – Creating Global Bonds

Lesson	Assessment	Group/ Individual	Formative/ Summative	Lesson Objective Assessed
1	STEM Research Notebook – Image Analysis *prompts*	Group	Formative	Recognize manifestations of climate change through photographic evidence analysis.
1	STEM Research Notebook – Hypothesis Development *prompts*	Group/Individual	Formative	Hypothesize the relationship between energy consumption and climate change.
1	Data Collection Table *handout*	Group/Individual	Formative	Identify various sources of energy utilized in their communities/ regions.
1	Blog Entry 1 *rubric*	Group/Individual	Formative	Hypothesize the relationship between energy consumption and climate change. Identify international partners with whom they can collaborate to analyze parallel data.
2	STEM Research Notebook – Claims/Evidence/Reasoning *graphic organizer prompts*	Group/Individual	Formative	Use data to identify themes of energy consumption and climate change across international contexts.
2	STEM Research Notebook – Problem Solving Activities *handout and prompts*	Group/Individual	Formative	Synthesize themes to create a series of strategies to facilitate more efficient energy consumption and climate change mitigation.

		Group/Individual	Formative	
2	Blog Entry 2 *rubric*		Formative	Develop communication strategies for use with international partners. Use problem-solving strategies to evaluate the utility and feasibility of strategies developed.
3	White Paper *rubric*	Group	Summative	Deliberate to consider the most effective means to communicate with members of scientific, governmental, and energy communities to share data and proposed solutions to challenges. Related to energy consumption and climate change, develop effective research presentations using data and collaboration techniques.
3	Presentation *rubric*	Group	Summative	Deliberate to consider the most effective means to communicate with members of scientific, governmental, and energy communities to share data and proposed solutions to challenges. Related to energy consumption and climate change, develop effective research presentations using data and collaboration techniques.

REFERENCES

Black, P., & Wiliam, D. (1998). Inside the black box: Raising standards through classroom assessment. *Phi Delta Kappan*, *80*(2), 139–148.

Black, P., Harrison, C., Lee, C., Marshall, B., & Wiliam, D. (2003). *Assessment for learning: Putting it into practice*. Open University Press.

Brookhart, S. M., & Nitko, A. J. (2008). *Assessment and grading in classrooms*. Pearson.

Popham, W. J. 2013. *Classroom assessment: What teachers need to know* (7th ed.). Pearson.

Sondergeld, T. A., Bell, C. A., & Leusner, D. M. (2010). Understanding how teachers engage in formative assessment. *Teaching and Learning*, *24*(2), 72–86.

CREATING GLOBAL BONDS – MODULE LESSONS

*Anthony Pellegrino, Jennifer Drake-Patrick, Brad Rankin,
Erin E. Peters-Burton, Janet B. Walton, and Carla C. Johnson*

Lesson Plan 1
Energy Consumption and Climate Change: At Home and Around the World

LESSON ONE SUMMARY

During this introductory lesson, students will gain an understanding of manifestations of climate change and hypothesize relationships between energy consumption and climate change. Further, students will collect data related to energy consumption and climate change in their communities and regions. Using those data, students will identify international partners with whom they can collaborate to analyze parallel data.

ESSENTIAL QUESTIONS

- How has climate change affected global environments?

- What energy sources are consumed in your community and region?

- What effects of climate change are most likely to impact your community and region?

- What are possible connections between energy consumption and climate change affecting your community or region?

ESTABLISHED GOALS/OBJECTIVES

At the conclusion of this lesson, students will be able to:

- recognize manifestations of climate change through photographic evidence analysis;

- identify various sources of energy utilized in their communities/regions;

DOI: 10.4324/9781003362371-8

- hypothesize the relationship between energy consumption and climate change;

- identify international partners with whom they can collaborate to analyze parallel data.

TIME REQUIRED

Six days (Days 1–6 in schedule; approximately 45 minutes each. Day 6 will also serve as an introduction to lesson plan 2.)

NECESSARY MATERIALS

Computer access to the internet for research and access to international school partners.

Table 6.1. Content Standards Addressed in STEM Road Map Module Lesson One

---

NEXT GENERATION SCIENCE STANDARDS

PERFORMANCE OBJECTIVES

HS-ESS2-4 Use a model to describe how variations in the flow of energy into and out of Earth's systems result in changes in climate.

HS-ESS3-5 Analyze geoscience data and the results from global climate models to make an evidence-based forecast of the current rate of global or regional climate change and associated future impacts to Earth systems.

HS-ESS3-6 Use a computational representation to illustrate the relationships among Earth systems and how those relationships are being modified due to human activity.

DISCIPLINARY CORE IDEAS

ESS2.D: Weather and Climate

- Changes in the atmosphere due to human activity have increased carbon dioxide concentrations and thus affect climate. (HS-ESS2-6; HS-ESS2-4)

- Current models predict that, although future regional climate changes will be complex and varied, average global temperatures will continue to rise. The outcomes predicted by global climate models strongly depend on the amounts of human-generated greenhouse gases added to the atmosphere each year and by the ways in which these gases are absorbed by the ocean and biosphere. (secondary to HS-ESS3-6)

ESS3.A: Natural Resources

- Resource availability has guided the development of human society. (HS-ESS3-1)

- All forms of energy production and other resource extraction have associated economic, social, environmental, and geopolitical costs and risks as well as benefits. New technologies and social regulations can change the balance of these factors. (HS-ESS3-2)

ESS3.C: Human Impacts on Earth Systems

- The sustainability of human societies and the biodiversity that supports them requires responsible management of natural resources. (HS-ESS3-3)

- Scientists and engineers can make major contributions by developing technologies that produce less pollution and waste and that preclude ecosystem degradation. (HS-ESS3-4)

ESS3.D: Global Climate Change

- Though the magnitudes of human impacts are greater than they have ever been, so too are human abilities to model, predict, and manage current and future impacts. (HS-ESS3-5)

- Through computer simulations and other studies, important discoveries are still being made about how the ocean, the atmosphere, and the biosphere interact and are modified in response to human activities. (HS-ESS3-6)

CROSSCUTTING CONCEPTS

Stability and Change

Change and rates of change can be quantified and modeled over very short or very long periods of time. Some system changes are irreversible.

Cause and Effect

Empirical evidence is required to differentiate between cause and correlation and make claims about specific causes and effects.

Systems and System Models

When investigating or describing a system, the boundaries and initial conditions of the system need to be defined and their inputs and outputs analyzed and described using models.

Connections to Engineering, Technology, and Applications of Science

Influence of Science, Engineering, and Technology on Society and the Natural World

Modern civilization depends on major technological systems.

New technologies can have deep impacts on society and the environment, including some that were not anticipated.

Connections to Nature of Science

Science is a Human Endeavor

Science is a result of human endeavors, imagination, and creativity.

SCIENCE AND ENGINEERING PRACTICES

Analyzing and Interpreting Data

- Analyze data using computational models in order to make valid and reliable scientific claims. (HS-ESS3-5)

Continued

Table 6.1. (*Continued*)

Using Mathematics and Computational Thinking

- Create a computational model or simulation of a phenomenon, designed device, process, or system. (HS-ESS3-3)

- Use a computational representation of phenomena or design solutions to describe and/or support claims and/or explanations. (HS-ESS3-6)

Constructing Explanations and Designing Solutions

- Construct an explanation based on valid and reliable evidence obtained from a variety of sources (including students' own investigations, models, theories, simulations, peer review) and the assumption that theories and laws that describe the natural world operate today as they did in the past and will continue to do so in the future. (HS-ESS3-1)

- Design or refine a solution to a complex real-world problem, based on scientific knowledge, student-generated sources of evidence, prioritized criteria, and tradeoff considerations. (HS-ESS3-4)

Engaging in Argument from Evidence

- Evaluate competing design solutions to a real-world problem based on scientific ideas and principles, empirical evidence, and logical arguments regarding relevant factors (e.g., economic, societal, environmental, ethical considerations). (HS-ESS3-2)

COMMON CORE MATHEMATICS STANDARDS
MATHEMATICS PRACTICES

MP1 Make sense of problems and persevere in solving them.

MP3 Construct viable arguments and critique the reasoning of others.

MP8 Look for and express regularity in repeated reasoning.

COMMON CORE ENGLISH/LANGUAGE ARTS STANDARDS
READING STANDARDS

RH 11-12.1 Cite specific textual evidence to support analysis of primary and secondary sources, connecting insights gained from specific details to an understanding of the text as a whole.

RH 11-12.2 Determine the central ideas or information of a primary or secondary source; provide an accurate summary that makes clear the relationships among the key details and ideas.

RH.11-12.3 Evaluate various explanations for actions or events and determine which explanation best accords with textual evidence, acknowledging where the text leaves matters uncertain.

RH 11-12.7 Integrate and evaluate multiple sources of information presented in diverse formats and media (e.g., visually, quantitatively, as well as in words) in order to address a question or solve a problem.

21ST CENTURY SKILLS

Creativity & Innovation, Critical Thinking & Problem Solving, Communication & Collaboration, Information Literacy, Media Literacy, ICT Literacy, Flexibility & Adaptability, Initiative & Self-Direction, Social & Cross-Cultural Skills, Productivity & Accountability, Leadership & Responsibility

---

Table 6.2. Key Vocabulary for Lesson One

Key Vocabulary*	Definition
Climate	The weather conditions prevailing in an area in general or over a long period.
Climate Change	A change in global or regional climate patterns; in particular, a change apparent from the mid to late 20th century onward and attributed largely to the increased levels of atmospheric carbon dioxide produced by the use of fossil fuels.
Fossil Fuel	A natural fuel such as coal or gas, formed in the geological past from the remains of living organisms.
Hypothesis	A supposition or proposed explanation made on the basis of limited evidence as a starting point for further investigation.
Renewable Energy	Energy from a source that is not depleted when used, such as wind or solar power.
Utility	The state of being useful, profitable, or beneficial.
Weather	The state of the atmosphere at a place and time as regards heat, dryness, sunshine, wind, rain, etc.
* Vocabulary terms are provided for both teacher and student use. Teachers may choose to introduce all or some terms to students.	

TEACHER BACKGROUND INFORMATION

Teachers should investigate ways to connect their students with international partners. Sites such as epals, Skype in the Classroom, Edmodo, globalclassroom, and iEARN-USA provide great starting points. The following Association for Supervision and Curriculum Development (ASCD) website is a clearing house for organizations that facilitate international connections, tools for collaborating, and ideas for projects (www.ascd.org/el/articles/resources-for-international-collaboration). Teachers should, however, take steps to establish these partnerships several weeks before commencement of the module as these partnerships can take time to align in terms of calendars, objectives, and prerequisite knowledge students need to participate. Additionally, through coordinated effort, teachers should pre-arrange student pairings. Ideally, this will include a parallel effort in which students are collecting and analyzing data from their respective communities to share during the second lesson. Doing so ahead of time will facilitate more efficient collaboration time.

Lesson Preparation

An article from Edutopia offers an overview for teachers new to working with teachers and students outside their schools: (www.edutopia.org/blog/pen-pals-in-21st-century-lisa-mims).

Learning Plan Components
Introductory Activity/Engagement

Days 1–2

Connections to the Challenge: Begin each day of this lesson by directing students' attention to the driving question for the module and challenge, asking "What is climate change? How has it affected global environments?" Hold a brief student discussion of how their learning contributed to their ability to create their plan for their innovation in the final challenge. You may wish to hold a class discussion, creating a class list of key ideas on chart paper or the board, or you may wish to have students create a STEM Research Notebook entry with this information.

Science Class

In the opening activity, small groups of students (two to three per group) are presented with several images from the following website: http://climate.nasa.gov/images-of-change#574-lake-mead-at-record-low

STEM Research Notebook Prompt

In their groups, students are to discern the general climate of the areas depicted in the images and discuss how climate change has potentially impacted these areas. Teachers may use a graphic organizer to support student inference-making, which is found at the end of this lesson plan. There is also an image analysis handout found at the end of this lesson plan that can help guide students in their analysis. Have students answer the following questions:

What patterns do you notice in the photos? Why do you think this is happening?

Following that activity, show or distribute the map of global energy consumption found at https://ourworldindata.org/worlds-energy-problem.

STEM Research Notebook Prompt

Allow students to make connections between energy use and climate change using the Global Energy Consumption graphic organizer found at the end of this lesson to help students make appropriate connections between the sources. Have students answer the following question:

Based on the data from the map of global energy consumption, what inferences can you make about human activities (lifestyle), characteristics of the country, and energy consumption?

During this time, teachers should also introduce students to the module challenge to work with international partners and create an action plan to address issues of energy consumption and climate change.

Mathematics Connections

Students can review the International Energy Agency's annual energy statistics document to explore energy consumption and production statistics in more detail. The 2021 report can be found at www.iea.org/reports/electricity-information-overview. *Using this report, students can predict future energy consumption based on past data.*

STEM Research Notebook Prompt

Choose two variables from the International Energy Agency's annual energy statistics document and document their trends from 1973 to 2013. Predict what the variable will be in the next 40 years. Explain to a partner how you have calculated this value. Answer the following question:

If the trends from 1973 to 2013 continue in the same linear pattern, would the Earth be able to sustain this amount of energy consumption for the next 200 years? Why or why not?

Teachers can review how to perform regressions on the TI-84 (see this YouTube video for a tutorial www.youtube.com/watch?v=LVnHpmbv7Yg and introduce advanced programs like Minitab or SPSS for larger data sets.

ELA Connections

Students should develop a written hypothesis connecting global energy consumption and climate change. There is a handout found at the end of this lesson to guide the students.

STEM Research Notebook Prompt

Based on your image analysis, your research into the locations of these images, and your review of global energy consumption data found at https://ourworldindata.org/worlds-energy-problem, develop a hypothesis about the connection between energy consumption and climate change. Use the following guide to help you through your hypothesis development.

Social Studies Connections

As a class, discuss how climate change might affect cultures, migration patterns, and conflict, specifically in areas where water is becoming increasingly scarce. The United Nations offers several resources related to this topic (see www.un.org/waterforlifedecade/scarcity.shtml). From this discussion and resource review, students will identify connections between areas of water scarcity and predict potential global conflict zones in future decades.

STEM Research Notebook Prompt

After reviewing the United Nations Water for Life website, answer the following question in your STEM Research Notebook:

What is the connection between areas of water scarcity and potential global conflict zones? How is climate change a factor in this connection?

Activity/Investigation

Days 3–4

Science Class

Following the introductory activities, students should form pairs to examine local and regional data related to energy sources and energy consumption. Typically, state environmental agencies and local energy utilities offer these data. The following website from the U.S. Energy Information Administration provides energy consumption, prices and expenditures, and energy production for each state – www.eia.gov/state/seds

STEM Research Notebook Prompt

Record the different types of data found on the U.S. Energy Information Administration website (www.eia.gov/state/seds). From your state of residence, choose one way to organize and represent the data for each of the following topics: energy consumption, prices and expenditures, and energy production. For an advanced version of this prompt, students can download the CSV data files, clean the files, and test for outliers. Students should answer the following question:

If you had to explain a comprehensive picture of the energy consumption, prices and expenditures, and energy production for your state, including all sources and descriptions, how would you organize the data?

Mathematics Connections

Students can compile energy source, consumption, and pricing data and graph it to track across time and identify trends in data. A Data Collection Guide is found at the end of this lesson to help students understand the key points of the task. Reviewing functions and graphs (i.e., linear, exponential, logarithmic, etc. – www.khanacademy. org/math/algebra-home/alg-linear-eq-func) will aid students in estimating where the trends are going and which type of regression to use.

ELA Connections

Students will research blog hosting platforms (see websites such as this one – http:// goinswriter.com/self-hosted-blog).

STEM Research Notebook Prompt

Reflect on your research about blogs to answer the following question in your STEM Research Notebook:

What did you find from your research about blogs to make them effective as communication tools?

Students will continue their research on local and regional data in the prior part of the lesson related to energy sources and energy consumption to create and write their first blog draft (Blog 1). Hand out the rubric for the Blog 1 task to the students and explain that their blog will be assessed on Evidence of Data Collection, Data Analysis, and Clarity of Communication to the Audience.

Social Studies Connections

Students will examine climate maps and almanac data to discern potential areas of the globe that may be impacted by climate change and those that may face similar challenges as those in their local or regional communities. Students will then compare these areas on a T-Chart or similarly purposed graphic organizer as noted below.

T-Chart

Local Impacts on Climate Change	Similar Impacts in Other Areas on Earth (note the location)

Explain

Days 3–5

Science Class

Explain that students should work with data collected in their STEM Research Notebook to develop a cohesive overview of their state energy consumption trends. They can create hypotheses such as differences in means and test them with appropriate statistical tests. Alternatively, they can analyze trends and use multiple regression to predict future trends. As in the Activity/Investigation portion of this lesson, students will explain connections they made between energy consumption and climate change.

Mathematics Connections

Work with students to support translating mathematical data from state energy consumption and climate change into graphs and tables to be added to Blog 1 and the white paper that is part of the final challenge.

ELA Connections

Organize the Global Partners previously identified in the Lesson Preparation and show students the choices they have for partners. As students identify the global partners they will work with in the future portions of the lessons, students should perform research to gather information about the region from where their partners come.

STEM Research Notebook Prompt

After you identify your global partner and gather information about this region, answer the following question in your STEM Research Notebook:

Where is your global partner located? What is it like living in this region?

This will include efforts to read fiction and non-fiction information about these areas to enhance cross-cultural understanding. Teachers will support this through explaining how students might find appropriate sources.

Social Studies Connections

By this point, teachers have already established potential international partners for the next phases of the project; however, allowing students to discover potential partners as well supports their understanding that climate change is a widespread problem beyond places such as California, Florida, Antarctica, or The Netherlands. Students will research the geography, economy, culture, and history of potential partner sites, and create a travel brochure for their identified region as a culminating activity.

STEM Research Notebook Prompt

Students should respond to the following prompt by writing individually in their STEM Research Notebooks and then discussing their ideas with a partner. Students should update their notebook entry based on what they learned from the conversation they had with their partner.

What is the geography, economy, culture and history of your global partner site?

Students should report on their global sites to the whole class.

Extend/Apply Knowledge

Days 5–6

Science Class

Students should communicate with their global partners about the challenge and the blog they will be collaboratively developing. Students should then finalize and share the blog draft with global partners for feedback. Students should share results in the same ways that scientists do – by connecting their evidence to their claims through reasoning. Students can use the inference graphic organizer found at the end of this lesson to help guide their thoughts. Student groups will also develop consensus as to what additional data they want to collect and collaborate with the international partners to determine what data the international partners will collect.

Blogs should be created as a product using the Engineering Design Process. The steps of the engineering process are:

- **Define:** Define the problem. What is the problem? How have others approached it? Identify the requirements.

- **Learn:** Brainstorm possible solutions and find the best solution.

- **Plan:** Do research, list materials needed, and identify steps you will take. Follow your plan and build a prototype.

- **Try**: Test the prototype. What works, what doesn't? What could you improve?

- **Decide:** Redesign to solve problems that came up in testing and retest.

- **Share:** Present it to others and let them give you feedback. After it has been critiqued, it often has to go back to the drawing table and be reconfigured and a new prototype is fashioned. Don't be discouraged if this happens. It is part of the process.

Mathematics Connections

In mathematics, students will examine data to identify gaps in data that may be included in the findings.

ELA Connections

Students will continue to finalize Blog 1.

Social Studies Connections

Students will research the history of their state (or the U.S. when appropriate) since 1973 and document it in their STEM Research Notebook. Students will use the state data they collected and contextualize it in terms of historical trends and policy that has

been enacted to influence energy consumption and climate change. This information will become part of the blog entry.

STEM Research Notebook Prompt

Answer the following question in your STEM Research Notebook by conducting some research:

How has the energy consumption trends you found for your state been reflected in the history of the state (or the U.S.)? What trends might have occurred to spur on high or low energy consumption?

Evaluate/Assessment

Image Analysis Activity

Hypothesis Development Activity (Days 1–2)

Data Collection (local and regional energy sources and consumption data, and effects of climate change in local and regional communities) (Days 3–4)

Blog 1 (Days 3–6)

Internet Resources

- Khan Academy tutorial on reviewing functions and graphs (i.e., linear, exponential, logarithmic, etc. – www.khanacademy.org/math/algebra-home/alg-linear-eq-func

- Blog Hosting platform – http://goinswriter.com/self-hosted-blog

- U.S. Energy Information Administration provides energy consumption, prices and expenditures, and energy production for each state – www.eia.gov/state/seds

- Global energy consumption data – https://ourworldindata.org/worlds-energy-problem

- The United Nations offers resources on conflict and water scarcity – www.un.org/waterforlifedecade/scarcity.shtml

- Tutorial for regression analysis on the TI-84 – www.youtube.com/watch?v=LVnHpmbv7Yg

- International Energy Agency's annual energy statistics – www.iea.org/reports/electricity-information-overview

- NASA's images of climate change – http://climate.nasa.gov/images-of-change#574-lake-mead-at-record-low

IMAGE ANALYSIS HANDOUT

Observation

Study the pairs of photographs from http://climate.nasa.gov/images-of-change#574-lake-mead-at-record-low. Identify three to four pairs of images on which you would like to focus. Do some additional research about the location these photographs were taken and use the steps below to guide you.

Step 1. Inference

A. Based on what you have observed in these pictures, what are the most striking changes you see?

_____

_____

_____

B. How might climate change have impacted the environment depicted in the photographs?

_____

_____

_____

Step 2. Questions

A. Based on your observations, where might these images be from? What leads you to come to that conclusion?

_____

_____

_____

B. Where could you find answers to how these places changed so dramatically?

_____

_____

_____

HYPOTHESIS DEVELOPMENT HANDOUT

Based on your image analysis, your research into the locations of these images, and your review of global energy consumption data found at https://ourworldindata.org/worlds-energy-problem, develop a hypothesis about the connection between energy consumption and climate change. Use the following guide to help you through your hypothesis development.

DEVELOPING A HYPOTHESIS

If _____ is changed by...
           (manipulated variable)

then _____ will...
           (responding variable)

because...

Sources Cited

DATA COLLECTION HANDOUT

To support data collection of local and regional energy resources and consumption, the following resource may be useful.

DATA COLLECTION GUIDE

Type of Data Collected	Source of Data	When Were These Data Collected?	From Whom Do These Data Come?	Questions These Data Will Answer

GRAPHIC ORGANIZER FOR INFERENCE-MAKING

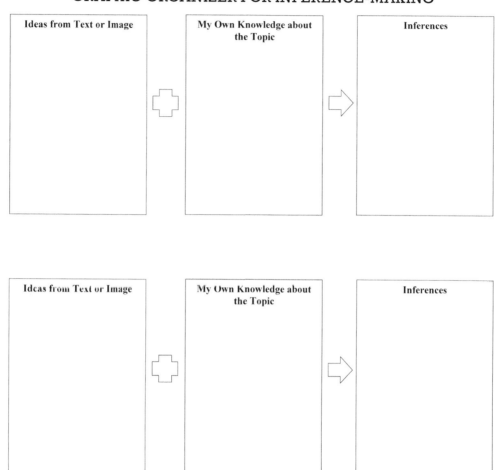

GRAPHIC ORGANIZER FOR ENERGY CONSUMPTION

Countries with Highest Energy Consumption	Common Characteristics of These Countries
Countries with the Lowest Energy Consumption	**Common Characteristics of These Countries**
Inferences about Energy Consumption and Lifestyle	

BLOG ENTRY 1 RUBRIC

	Expert	Competent	Emerging	Did not Meet Expectations	Score	Comments
Evidence of Data Collection	Data presented in blog was directly related to energy consumption and climate change in local/regional areas and background knowledge was correctly cited.	Data presented in blog was directly related to energy consumption and climate change in local/regional areas. Limited background knowledge was cited.	Data presented in blog was not directly related to energy consumption and climate change in local/regional areas. Any data presented were not connected to background knowledge.	Little or no data were presented. No evidence of using outside sources to inform the blog posting.		
Data Organization	Data were clearly organized and connected to the topic throughout the blog posting.	Data were clearly organized, but connections between topics was limited throughout the blog posting.	Data were minimally organized. No connections between topics was evident.	Data were not organized systematically.		
Communication of Results and Conclusion	Results and conclusion were constructed as an argument, supported clearly by evidence and reasoning found in the data collection.	Results and conclusion were communicated, but not constructed as an argument, supported clearly by evidence and reasoning found in the data collection.	Results were communicated, but a conclusion was not constructed.	Neither results nor conclusion were communicated.		

Lesson Plan 2
Making International Connections to Identify Relationships between Energy Consumption and Climate Change

LESSON TWO SUMMARY

In this series of activities, students will develop their international partnerships, compare data from their own communities with those from their international partners, and look for common themes of energy consumption and climate change to facilitate the development of mitigation strategies advocated by both the scientific and policy communities. This lesson will culminate in the collaboratively written blog posting chronicling the partners' efforts and ideas. This work will lead up to the final lesson, which challenges students to develop a more formal white paper with recommended strategies and a presentation of their findings.

ESSENTIAL QUESTIONS

- What similarities and differences are evident in energy consumption and climate change patterns across international contexts?

- What strategies can be employed to support more efficient energy use and climate change mitigation?

ESTABLISHED GOALS/OBJECTIVES

By the end of this lesson, students will be able to:

- develop communication strategies for use with international partners;

- use data to identify themes of energy consumption and climate change across international contexts;

- synthesize themes to create a series of strategies to facilitate more efficient energy consumption and climate change mitigation;

- use problem-solving strategies to evaluate the utility and feasibility of strategies developed.

TIME REQUIRED

7 days (about 45-minute periods; Days 6–12 in the schedule)

NECESSARY MATERIALS

Internet access and conferencing software for synchronous or asynchronous communication. This may come in the form of an annotated PowerPoint or more sophisticated software that allows synchronous or asynchronous conferencing.

Table 6.3. Content Standards Addressed in STEM Road Map Module Lesson Two

---

NEXT GENERATION SCIENCE STANDARDS

PERFORMANCE OBJECTIVES

HS-ESS3-3 Create a computational simulation to illustrate the relationships among management of natural resources, the sustainability of human populations, and biodiversity.

HS-ESS2-4 Use a model to describe how variations in the flow of energy into and out of Earth's systems result in changes in climate.

HS-ESS3-5 Analyze geoscience data and the results from global climate models to make an evidence-based forecast of the current rate of global or regional climate change and associated future impacts to Earth systems.

HS-ESS3-6 Use a computational representation to illustrate the relationships among Earth systems and how those relationships are being modified due to human activity.

DISCIPLINARY CORE IDEAS

ESS2.D: Weather and Climate

- Changes in the atmosphere due to human activity have increased carbon dioxide concentrations and thus affect climate. (HS-ESS2-6; HS-ESS2-4)

- Current models predict that, although future regional climate changes will be complex and varied, average global temperatures will continue to rise. The outcomes predicted by global climate models strongly depend on the amounts of human-generated greenhouse gases added to the atmosphere each year and by the ways in which these gases are absorbed by the ocean and biosphere. (secondary to HS-ESS3-6)

ESS3.A: Natural Resources

- Resource availability has guided the development of human society. (HS-ESS3-1)

- All forms of energy production and other resource extraction have associated economic, social, environmental, and geopolitical costs and risks as well as benefits. New technologies and social regulations can change the balance of these factors. (HS-ESS3-2)

ESS3.C: Human Impacts on Earth Systems

- The sustainability of human societies and the biodiversity that supports them requires responsible management of natural resources. (HS-ESS3-3)

- Scientists and engineers can make major contributions by developing technologies that produce less pollution and waste and that preclude ecosystem degradation. (HS-ESS3-4)

ESS3.D: Global Climate Change

- Though the magnitudes of human impacts are greater than they have ever been, so too are human abilities to model, predict, and manage current and future impacts. (HS-ESS3-5)

- Through computer simulations and other studies, important discoveries are still being made about how the ocean, the atmosphere, and the biosphere interact and are modified in response to human activities. (HS-ESS3-6)

ETS1.B: Developing Possible Solutions

- When evaluating solutions, it is important to take into account a range of constraints, including cost, safety, reliability, and aesthetics, and to consider social, cultural, and environmental impacts. (secondary to HS-ESS3-2; secondary HS-ESS3-4)

CROSSCUTTING CONCEPTS

Stability and Change

Change and rates of change can be quantified and modeled over very short or very long periods of time. Some system changes are irreversible.

Cause and Effect

Empirical evidence is required to differentiate between cause and correlation and make claims about specific causes and effects.

Systems and System Models

When investigating or describing a system, the boundaries and initial conditions of the system need to be defined and their inputs and outputs analyzed and described using models.

Connections to Engineering, Technology, and Applications of Science

Influence of Science, Engineering, and Technology on Society and the Natural World

Modern civilization depends on major technological systems.

New technologies can have deep impacts on society and the environment, including some that were not anticipated.

Connections to Nature of Science

Science is a Human Endeavor

Science is a result of human endeavors, imagination, and creativity.

SCIENCE AND ENGINEERING PRACTICES

Analyzing and Interpreting Data

- Analyze data using computational models in order to make valid and reliable scientific claims. (HS-ESS3-5)

Continued

Table 6.3. (*Continued*)

Using Mathematics and Computational Thinking

- Create a computational model or simulation of a phenomenon, designed device, process, or system. (HS-ESS3-3)

- Use a computational representation of phenomena or design solutions to describe and/or support claims and/or explanations. (HS-ESS3-6)

Constructing Explanations and Designing Solutions

- Construct an explanation based on valid and reliable evidence obtained from a variety of sources (including students' own investigations, models, theories, simulations, peer review) and the assumption that theories and laws that describe the natural world operate today as they did in the past and will continue to do so in the future. (HS-ESS3-1)

- Design or refine a solution to a complex real-world problem, based on scientific knowledge, student-generated sources of evidence, prioritized criteria, and tradeoff considerations. (HS-ESS3-4)

Engaging in Argument from Evidence

- Evaluate competing design solutions to a real-world problem based on scientific ideas and principles, empirical evidence, and logical arguments regarding relevant factors (e.g., economic, societal, environmental, ethical considerations). (HS-ESS3-2)

COMMON CORE MATHEMATICS STANDARDS
MATHEMATICS PRACTICES

MP1 Make sense of problems and persevere in solving them.

MP3 Construct viable arguments and critique the reasoning of others.

MP8 Look for and express regularity in repeated reasoning.

MATHEMATICS CONTENT

HSA-REI.B.3 Solve linear equations and inequalities in one variable, including equations with coefficients represented by letters.

HSA-REI.A.2 Solve simple rational and radical equations in one variable, and give examples showing how extraneous solutions may arise.

COMMON CORE ENGLISH/LANGUAGE ARTS STANDARDS
READING STANDARDS

RH 11-12.1 Cite specific textual evidence to support analysis of primary and secondary sources, connecting insights gained from specific details to an understanding of the text as a whole.

RH 11-12.2 Determine the central ideas or information of a primary or secondary source; provide an accurate summary that makes clear the relationships among the key details and ideas.

RH.11-12.3 Evaluate various explanations for actions or events and determine which explanation best accords with textual evidence, acknowledging where the text leaves matters uncertain.

RH 11-12.7 Integrate and evaluate multiple sources of information presented in diverse formats and media (e.g., visually, quantitatively, as well as in words) in order to address a question or solve a problem.

> **21ST CENTURY SKILLS**
>
> Global Awareness, Civic Literacy, Creativity & Innovation, Critical Thinking & Problem Solving, Communication & Collaboration, Information Literacy, Media Literacy, ICT Literacy, Flexibility & Adaptability, Initiative & Self-Direction, Social & Cross-Cultural Skills, Productivity & Accountability, Leadership & Responsibility

Table 6.4. Key Vocabulary for Lesson Two

Key Vocabulary*	Definition
Mitigation	The action of reducing the severity, seriousness, or painfulness of something
Strategy	A large, overall plan that is future-oriented
Tactic	Plan, task, or procedure usually carried out as part of the bigger strategy
Theme	A recurring idea found in data (or another kind of text); a central topic
* Vocabulary terms are provided for both teacher and student use. Teachers may choose to introduce all or some terms to students.	

TEACHER BACKGROUND INFORMATION

The teacher should spend considerable time in this lesson guiding students in their interactions with their international partners. As such, teachers should communicate with the teachers of the international partner students to establish clear expectations. Developing a brief overview email with objectives, outcomes, and a timetable would be beneficial. The first few days of this lesson are designed to give partners opportunities to learn about each other's contexts, and establish common understanding and shared goals of the project. Ideally, however, the international partner teachers will have the opportunity to get their students to collect similar data about their communities to facilitate the collaboration needed for this lesson. Having the teachers aligned in this effort will be useful to support this work.

In addition to having a working relationship with the international partners for this module, it is important to be familiar with the types of data available for climate change indicators and energy consumption information. In Lesson One, students began collecting and analyzing data for Blog Entry 1. Teachers can support students in building complexity for their blogs and eventually the white papers by helping students seek additional reliable resources from the internet to elaborate on the data analysis and findings from Blog 1 or to add additional variables that give a more complex picture of energy consumption and climate change.

Lesson Preparation

During this part of the lesson, the teacher will work to establish partnerships between their students and those from the international schools. The following Association for Supervision and Curriculum Development (ASCD) website is a clearing house for

organizations that facilitate international connections, tools for collaborating, and ideas for projects (www.ascd.org/el/articles/resources-for-international-collaboration). This Education World article explains connection sites such as Schoolworld Internet Education and ideas for internet global collaborations – www.educationworld.com/a_tech/tech089.shtml. Partnerships will vary depending on the level of interest from other schools to participate and numbers of students with each participating teacher. Teachers, therefore, should be flexible in terms of numbers of students in each partnership. Two pairs of students (one local and one international) represent the ideal configuration, but other group sizes are acceptable as well.

Before launching into communicating with international partners, teachers should ensure that student pairs have collected and compiled their local or state community data relating to energy consumption and climate change and have a clear sense of the project objectives. Additionally, teachers should allow students to spend time researching their international partners' region. This activity might not focus on energy consumption and climate change in the region, but rather culture, education, and daily living experiences. This effort will surely support the cross-cultural understanding needed in a project such as this.

Teachers should also be familiar with infographics and reliable resources describing infographics. The following websites may be helpful:

- What is an infographic? – www.technokids.com/blog/technology-integration/what-is-an-infographic

- What are infographics and why are they important? – www.instantshift.com/2011/03/25/what-are-infographics-and-why-are-they-important

- Designing infographics at Lynda.com – www.lynda.com/Illustrator-tutorials/Designing-Infographic/160274-2.html

- Designing infographics at Canva – www.canva.com

- 10 steps to designing an infographic – www.ebsco.com/blogs/novelist/10-tips-great-infographic

- The do's and don'ts of designing infographics, *Smashing Magazine* – www.smashingmagazine.com/2011/10/the-dos-and-donts-of-infographic-design

Learning Plan Components
Introductory Activity/Engagement

Days 6–7

Connections to the Challenge: Begin each day of this lesson by directing students' attention to the driving question for the module and challenge, asking "What trends are emerging from your data collection and analysis about energy consumption? What connections are you finding between energy consumption and climate change over the past 50 years?" Hold a brief student discussion of how their learning in the lesson(s) contributed to their ability to create their plan for their innovation in the final challenge. You may wish to hold a class discussion, creating a class list of key ideas on chart paper or the board, or you may wish to have students create a STEM Research Notebook entry with this information.

This lesson will culminate in the collaboratively written blog posting chronicling the partners' efforts and ideas. It begins with each class contributing to data collection on issues related to energy. In this lesson, international partners join in the current classroom discussion (virtually or possibly by videoconferencing over the internet) to discern energy consumption and climate change challenges felt across contexts. This work will lead up to the final lesson, which challenges students to develop a more formal white paper with recommended strategies and a presentation of their findings.

Science Class

STEM Research Notebook Prompt

Students should develop a brief report of the data collected from the first lesson regarding local and/or state community energy consumption and climate change. Students should be sure to include the evidence and reasoning to support the claims. There is a graphic organizer to facilitate the organization of student claims, evidence, and reasoning found at the end of this lesson. Answer these questions in the STEM Research Notebook along with supporting notes:

> *What are your research questions about energy consumption and climate change over time?*
>
> *What claim have you made from the analysis of the data?*
>
> *What evidence is there to support your claim?*
>
> *What are the reasons (scientific principles) that link your evidence to your claim?*

Students should introduce this report to the international partners as a means to develop a shared understanding of the project.

Mathematics Connections

Begin by displaying the STEM Research Notebook Prompt found below for the students. Have students conduct a brief internet search for reliable resources. Students could work individually or in pairs to complete the STEM Research Notebook prompt.

STEM Research Notebook Prompt

Using reliable resources you found on the internet, explain the key features of an infographic and why infographics are used.

Once the students have background in the key features of an infographic, students should create infographics to display the findings of the data to add to the brief report from science class.

ELA Connections

Revise and edit Blog 1 and the infographic for clarity and readability. The final draft of the report and infographic should include a list of the data the international partners will be collecting. Students should communicate with the international partners to determine the resources available and topics on which the local and international groups may be able to collaborate and compare data.

Social Studies Connections

Research the geography, economy, and culture of the region from where the international partners come. This information should be included in the report and on the infographic for discussion with the international partners. The international partners can provide feedback to the group on the accuracy of the research.

Activity/Investigation

Day 8

Science Class

Arrange and execute initial international partner exchanges. This exchange might include sharing the report and infographic of local and regional energy consumption and climate concerns, or using a platform such as PowerPoint to offer a summary thereof. In situations where synchronous meetings are possible, arrange a meeting on a media platform (e.g., Google Hangouts) to discuss data collection findings.

After the first (synchronous or asynchronous) meeting with international partners, students should begin to compare data for areas of overlap and differences with respect to energy consumption and climate change. For example, students may compare the amount of electricity consumption per household and the types and amounts of electronic devices in the average house in each region. Students may also want to compare behaviors around electronic devices such as leaving on the television even though no one is in the room, or turning off lights or unplugging chargers when not being used.

STEM Research Notebook prompt

After meeting with international partners, students should record they key points in the conversation by answering this question:

What are areas of overlap of your data with your international partner's data?

What are some different types of data that you and your international partner are collecting?

What might be some fruitful topics related to energy consumption and climate change that can be compared between your two groups?

What data might be needed to help bridge a gap between what you are collecting and what your international partners are collecting?

Mathematics Connections

Compare data between both groups of students and look to align topics for further study. Data might be compared about specific energy use from 1973–2013 and future projections.

ELA Connections

Organize notes from data comparison and data sources across contexts. This activity will be useful in problem-solving activities in science class where students are asked to identify three problems they have identified from their research and data collection.

Social Studies Connections

Students will examine the data from the international partners and discern any commonalities between the sources of data, the role(s) of the regulatory agencies, utility companies, and energy consumers. Similarly, students should share the data the local group collected with the international partners for review. Students should consider similarities and differences. Students will keep notes in their STEM Research Notebooks to use in problem-solving activities.

In addition to examining the data provided by the international partners, students should research internet resources regarding energy consumption habits in the regions of the international partners. Students should communicate what they find on the internet and confirm or refine with the international partners.

Explain

Days 9–11

Science Class

Organize student groups to engage in activity to discern the nature of the challenges the local and international partner communities have related to energy consumption

and climate change across contexts. Teachers will use this activity to help students identify three challenges or problems (common to both partner communities) that they would like to address. A Problem Solving Activity Guide is provided at the end of the lesson to help guide students in identifying three problems and explaining the needed information to address the problems. Blog 2 will be focused on these three problems, the potential solutions (claims), and the evidence that supports the potential solution.

Mathematics Connections

Teachers can support the science activity, helping students identify and analyze data that is common to both partner communities. This activity will inform how students ultimately determine which problems are most important and feasible to address.

ELA Connections

Use the problem-solving activity template to practice problem-solving strategies related to fictional or non-fictional dilemmas. This practice opportunity will inform how students ultimately determine which problems are most important and feasible to address.

Social Studies Connections

Use the problem-solving activity template to practice problem-solving strategies related to historical dilemmas such as Truman's decision to use the atomic bomb during World War II. This practice opportunity will inform how students ultimately determine which problems are most important and feasible to address.

Websites to help students with background information on Truman's decision include:

- The Decision to Drop the Bomb – www.ushistory.org/us/51g.asp

- No Other Choice – http://nationalinterest.org/feature/no-other-choice-why-truman-dropped-the-atomic-bomb-japan-13504

Extend/Apply Knowledge

Days 11–12

Science Class

From the three common challenges or problems identified, students should develop proposed solutions for each, linking the recommendation with evidence found in the data. Share these with international partners. Students should write Blog Entry 2 from the problem-solving activities and proposed solutions. There is a rubric found at the end of this lesson to guide the writing.

Mathematics Connections

Students should use data collected from each partner to discern the feasibility of addressing the challenges identified by the partners. Students should discuss any clarification or issues with the international partners.

ELA Connections

Students should review Blog Entry 2 in terms of problem-solving activities and proposed solutions for communication clarity and accuracy. Students could trade the blogs across partner groups and edit each other's blogs.

Social Studies Connections

Consider geographic, cultural, and economic implications of addressing the challenges to be included in the blog entry. This research may culminate in a short position paper that can be included in the second blog entry.

Evaluate/Assessment

Claims/Evidence/Reasoning Graphic Organizer

Problem-Solving Activities

Blog Entry 2 Rubric

Internet Resources

- What is an infographic? – www.technokids.com/blog/technology-integration/ what-is-an-infographic

- What are infographics and why are they important? – www.instantshift. com/2011/03/25/what-are-infographics-and-why-are-they-important

- Designing infographics at Lynda.com – www.lynda.com/Illustrator-tutorials/ Designing-Infographic/160274-2.html

- 10 steps to designing an infographic – www.fastcodesign.com/1670019/10-steps-to-designing-an-amazing-infographic

- The do's and don'ts of designing infographics, *Smashing Magazine* – www. smashingmagazine.com/2011/10/the-dos-and-donts-of-infographic-design/

CLAIMS/EVIDENCE/REASONING GRAPHIC ORGANIZER

Problem/Question:

Original Claim:

	Evidence	Reasoning
1		
2		
3		

Evidence Number	Rebuttal	Valid	Rationale

Conclusion:

PROBLEM SOLVING ACTIVITY GUIDE

Problem	Understand	Plan
	• What do you know? • What do you need to know?	• What strategy will you use to solve this problem?
	Solve • Show all your steps	**Check** • Did you answer the question? • Is your answer reasonable?

BLOG ENTRY 2 RUBRIC

	Expert	Competent	Emerging	Did not Meet Expectations	Score	Comments
Evidence of Data Collection	Data presented in blog was directly related to energy consumption and climate change in local/regional areas and background knowledge was correctly cited.	Data presented in blog was directly related to energy consumption and climate change in local/regional areas. Limited background knowledge was cited.	Data presented in blog was not directly related to energy consumption and climate change in local/regional areas. Any data presented were not connected to background knowledge.	Little or no data were presented. No evidence of using outside sources to inform blog posting.		
Data Organization	Data were clearly organized and connected to the topic throughout the blog posting.	Data were clearly organized, but connections between topics was limited throughout the blog posting.	Data were minimally organized. No connections between topics was evident.	Data were not organized systematically.		
Evidence of Problem Solving	Challenges and proposed solutions were clearly identified. Feasibility for proposed solutions was included.	Challenges and proposed solutions were clearly identified. Feasibility for proposed solutions was included, but lacked clarity and direct connection to proposed solutions.	Challenges and proposed solutions were identified. Feasibility for proposed solutions was not included, but lacked clarity and direct connection to proposed solutions.	Challenges and proposed solutions were not identified. Feasibility for proposed solutions was not included.		
Communication of Results and Conclusion	Results and conclusion were constructed as an argument, supported clearly by evidence and reasoning found in the data collection.	Results and conclusion were communicated, but not constructed as an argument, supported clearly by evidence and reasoning found in the data collection.	Results were communicated, but a conclusion was not constructed.	Neither results nor conclusion were communicated.		

6

Lesson Plan 3
Using Data to Impact Energy Consumption and Climate Change

LESSON THREE SUMMARY

In this series of lessons, students will synthesize their data analysis, challenges, or problems they have identified, along with their proposed solutions to develop a white paper and presentation to share their findings and ideas as indicated in the final challenge.

ESSENTIAL QUESTIONS

What are effective means to share data and affect change in scientific, governmental, and energy communities?

ESTABLISHED GOALS/OBJECTIVES

By the end of the lesson students should be able to:

- deliberate to consider the most effective means to communicate with members of scientific, governmental, and energy communities to share data and proposed solutions to challenges related to energy consumption and climate change;

- develop effective research presentations using data and collaboration techniques.

TIME REQUIRED

13 days (approximately 45 minutes each; Days 13–25 in the schedule. During days 13–17 students will largely focus on the development of their white paper. During days 18–22 students will focus on developing their presentations. The final two days of this lesson will be for formal presentations).

NECESSARY MATERIALS

Internet access and conferencing software for synchronous or asynchronous communication. This may come in the form of an annotated PowerPoint or more sophisticated software that allows synchronous or asynchronous conferencing.

Table 6.5. Content Standards Addressed in STEM Road Map Module Lesson Three

---

NEXT GENERATION SCIENCE STANDARDS
PERFORMANCE OBJECTIVES

HS-ESS3-3 Create a computational simulation to illustrate the relationships among management of natural resources, the sustainability of human populations, and biodiversity.

HS-ESS2-4 Use a model to describe how variations in the flow of energy into and out of Earth's systems result in changes in climate.

HS-ESS3-5 Analyze geoscience data and the results from global climate models to make an evidence-based forecast of the current rate of global or regional climate change and associated future impacts to Earth systems.

HS-ESS3-6 Use a computational representation to illustrate the relationships among Earth systems and how those relationships are being modified due to human activity.

DISCIPLINARY CORE IDEAS
ESS2.D: Weather and Climate

- Changes in the atmosphere due to human activity have increased carbon dioxide concentrations and thus affect climate. (HS-ESS2-6; HS-ESS2-4)

- Current models predict that, although future regional climate changes will be complex and varied, average global temperatures will continue to rise. The outcomes predicted by global climate models strongly depend on the amounts of human-generated greenhouse gases added to the atmosphere each year and by the ways in which these gases are absorbed by the ocean and biosphere. (secondary to HS-ESS3-6)

ESS3.A: Natural Resources

- Resource availability has guided the development of human society. (HS-ESS3-1)

- All forms of energy production and other resource extraction have associated economic, social, environmental, and geopolitical costs and risks as well as benefits. New technologies and social regulations can change the balance of these factors. (HS-ESS3-2)

ESS3.C: Human Impacts on Earth Systems

- The sustainability of human societies and the biodiversity that supports them requires responsible management of natural resources. (HS-ESS3-3)

- Scientists and engineers can make major contributions by developing technologies that produce less pollution and waste and that preclude ecosystem degradation. (HS-ESS3-4)

ESS3.D: Global Climate Change

- Though the magnitudes of human impacts are greater than they have ever been, so too are human abilities to model, predict, and manage current and future impacts. (HS-ESS3-5)

- Through computer simulations and other studies, important discoveries are still being made about how the ocean, the atmosphere, and the biosphere interact and are modified in response to human activities. (HS-ESS3-6)

ETS1.B: Developing Possible Solutions

- When evaluating solutions, it is important to take into account a range of constraints, including cost, safety, reliability, and aesthetics, and to consider social, cultural, and environmental impacts. (secondary to HS-ESS3-2; secondary HS-ESS3-4)

CROSSCUTTING CONCEPTS

Stability and Change

Change and rates of change can be quantified and modeled over very short or very long periods of time. Some system changes are irreversible.

Cause and Effect

Empirical evidence is required to differentiate between cause and correlation and make claims about specific causes and effects.

Systems and System Models

When investigating or describing a system, the boundaries and initial conditions of the system need to be defined and their inputs and outputs analyzed and described using models.

Connections to Engineering, Technology, and Applications of Science

Influence of Science, Engineering, and Technology on Society and the Natural World

Modern civilization depends on major technological systems.

New technologies can have deep impacts on society and the environment, including some that were not anticipated.

Connections to Nature of Science

Science is a Human Endeavor

Science is a result of human endeavors, imagination, and creativity.

SCIENCE AND ENGINEERING PRACTICES

Analyzing and Interpreting Data

- Analyze data using computational models in order to make valid and reliable scientific claims. (HS-ESS3-5)

Using Mathematics and Computational Thinking

- Create a computational model or simulation of a phenomenon, designed device, process, or system. (HS-ESS3-3)

- Use a computational representation of phenomena or design solutions to describe and/or support claims and/or explanations. (HS-ESS3-6)

Continued

Table 6.5. (*Continued*)

> *Constructing Explanations and Designing Solutions*
>
> - Construct an explanation based on valid and reliable evidence obtained from a variety of sources (including students' own investigations, models, theories, simulations, peer review) and the assumption that theories and laws that describe the natural world operate today as they did in the past and will continue to do so in the future. (HS-ESS3-1)
>
> - Design or refine a solution to a complex real-world problem, based on scientific knowledge, student-generated sources of evidence, prioritized criteria, and tradeoff considerations. (HS-ESS3-4)
>
> *Engaging in Argument from Evidence*
>
> - Evaluate competing design solutions to a real-world problem based on scientific ideas and principles, empirical evidence, and logical arguments regarding relevant factors (e.g., economic, societal, environmental, ethical considerations). (HS-ESS3-2)
>
> ## COMMON CORE MATHEMATICS STANDARDS
>
> ## MATHEMATICS PRACTICES
>
> MP1 Make sense of problems and persevere in solving them.
>
> MP3 Construct viable arguments and critique the reasoning of others.
>
> MP8 Look for and express regularity in repeated reasoning.
>
> ## MATHEMATICS CONTENT
>
> HSA-REI.B.3 Solve linear equations and inequalities in one variable, including equations with coefficients represented by letters.
>
> HSA-REI.A.2 Solve simple rational and radical equations in one variable, and give examples showing how extraneous solutions may arise.
>
> ## COMMON CORE ELA STANDARDS
>
> *Reading Standards*
>
> RH 11-12.1 Cite specific textual evidence to support analysis of primary and secondary sources, connecting insights gained from specific details to an understanding of the text as a whole.
>
> RH 11-12.2 Determine the central ideas or information of a primary or secondary source; provide an accurate summary that makes clear the relationships among the key details and ideas.
>
> RH.11-12.3 Evaluate various explanations for actions or events and determine which explanation best accords with textual evidence, acknowledging where the text leaves matters uncertain.
>
> RH 11-12.7 Integrate and evaluate multiple sources of information presented in diverse formats and media (e.g., visually, quantitatively, as well as in words) in order to address a question or solve a problem.
>
> ## 21ST CENTURY SKILLS
>
> Global Awareness, Civic Literacy, Creativity & Innovation, Critical Thinking & Problem Solving, Communication & Collaboration, Information Literacy, Media Literacy, ICT Literacy, Flexibility & Adaptability, Initiative & Self-Direction, Social & Cross-Cultural Skills, Productivity & Accountability, Leadership & Responsibility

Table 6.6. Key Vocabulary in Lesson Three

Key Vocabulary	Definition
Regulatory Agency	A public author or government agency responsible for exercising authority over some area of human activity in a supervisory capacity.
White Paper	An authoritative report or guide helping readers understand an issue, solve a problem, or make a decision. White papers typically include an overview of the issue and research-based recommendations to address the issue.
* Vocabulary terms are provided for both teacher and student use. Teachers may choose to introduce all or some terms to students.	

TEACHER BACKGROUND INFORMATION

The teacher should help guide students in exploring ways to effectively disseminate their data. In the scientific community, it is very important to understand how to communicate data for public consumption, as one needs to provide enough evidence to convince an audience, but not overwhelm them or be too technical. The early sessions of this lesson focus on developing a white paper from information that partners have already compiled and explained in two blog entries, as well as other class activities such as problem-solving activities. To transition toward developing a white paper from those data and artifacts, defining the parameters and expectations of a white paper and sharing examples is valuable. The USDA prepared a white paper that focuses specifically on climate change (search "Climate Change Science White Paper" from USDA to easily access the PDF). Likewise, the internet includes many generic white paper templates that include basic elements of a white paper. For the purposes of this module, the teacher should consider the audience to be informed and concerned citizens, thus challenging students to develop the white papers in an informative and clear expository format. It is recommended too that students get involved in researching for themselves other audiences, such as policymakers or business leaders, who might be interested in this topic.

The second portion of this lesson involves developing a presentation. Like the transition to developing a white paper, students benefit from examples. One challenging presentation format is Pecha Kucha (see www.pechakucha.org for more information). Briefly, this format is designed to maximize audience engagement and avoid typical pitfalls of long, tedious, and pedantic presentations. Taking students through the guidelines of Pecha Kucha may help them in their design and challenge them to develop effective presentations. Additionally, the TED blog offers a great post about developing presentation slides that help presenters communicate their ideas effectively (see http://blog.ted.com/10-tips-for-better-slide-decks). Although not specifically aligned to Pecha Kucha, the ideas work in concert.

Lesson Preparation

Preparation for the activities in this lesson involves establishing expectations for the white paper and the final presentation. As noted above, providing students with examples of formats for these two summative artifacts will allow partners to thrive in developing creative and informative ways to share the information they have worked to analyze.

Learning Plan Components
Introductory Activity/Engagement

Day 13

Connections to the Challenge: Begin each day of this lesson by directing students' attention to the driving question for the module and challenge, asking "How can complex topics such as energy consumption and climate change be communicated clearly? What experiences have you had that clarified complex topics?" Hold a brief student discussion of how their learning in the lesson(s) contributed to their ability to create their plan for their innovation in the final challenge. You may wish to hold a class discussion, creating a class list of key ideas on chart paper or the board, or you may wish to have students create a STEM Research Notebook entry with this information.

Science Class

Review Pecha Kucha guidelines and examples. As a whole class, discuss content and format. Relate how the Pecha Kucha guidelines are expectations in the rubric found at the end of this lesson.

Mathematics Connections

Update infographics based on collaboration with international partners to enhance final presentation example.

ELA Connections

Review the TED Blog guidelines for quality presentations (http://blog.ted.com/10-tips-for-better-slide-decks). Begin discussions of what to include and exclude in final presentation.

Social Studies Connections

Add social studies elements to infographics. This should include very brief writings on sociocultural and economic impacts of climate change. The writing here aligns with that which will be included in the white paper, but is far more concise and pointed to maintain the aesthetic of the infographic.

Activity/Investigation, Part I

Days 14–15

Science Class

Finalize data analysis and recommendations to be included in the white paper.

Mathematics Connections

Create infographics to enhance white paper.

ELA Connections

While continuing to work with international partners, draft the white paper. Share drafts with international partners.

Social Studies Connections

Focus on adding contextual elements of local and international partner communities to the white paper.

Activity/Investigation, Part II

Days 16–17

Science Class

Design and develop Pecha Kucha-style presentation with international partners.

Mathematics Connections

Create different data displays for Pecha Kucha presentation.

ELA Connections

Work to revise and edit presentation for readability and adherence to time and format expectations.

Social Studies Connections

Find and add images related to energy consumption and climate change to be included in the presentation. Ensure proper citation, captioning, and formatting of these images.

Explain

Days 17–20

Science Class

Review the USDA climate change white paper. Discuss scientific arguments, content, and format.

STEM Research Notebook Prompt

After reviewing the USDA climate change white paper, answer the following questions:

What claims are found in the USDA climate change white paper?

What is the evidence that backs up each of those claims?

What scientific principles (reasoning) explain why the evidence links with the claims?

Mathematics Connections

Explain how data informs policy recommendations. Create data-rich infographics to enhance the climate change white paper.

ELA Connections

Review the USDA climate change white paper. Discuss quality of the arguments, readability, and intended audience. Use this time to review the format for these types of papers, which typically include contextual background, relevant research, recommendations, and implications.

Social Studies Connections

Research recent energy consumption or climate change policy in the news. This may include recent data reports, regulations, or more general news stories related to the topics. Ask students to look for trends in these resources.

Extend/Apply Knowledge

Days 20–23

Science Class and Mathematics, ELA, and Social Studies Connections

Explain your findings and recommendations about energy consumption and climate change in a white paper and formal presentation.

Research to find two relevant groups beyond informed and concerned citizens who would benefit from hearing the presentation or reading the white paper. Consider, for example, local and regional community groups and business leaders, regulatory agencies, and policymakers in settings that include those of international partners. Work to consider how to best share findings and recommendations with these audiences.

STEM Research Notebook Prompt

After your research on finding other relevant audiences for the white paper and presentation, answer the following questions:

Beyond concerned citizens, what other groups would be relevant audiences for your work in this module? Why might they be a good audience? What would they get from your work?

Evaluate/Assessment

White Paper

Presentation

Internet Resources

- TED Blog guidelines for quality presentations – http://blog.ted.com/10-tips-for-better-slide-decks

- Pecha Kucha presentation guidelines – www.pechakucha.org

WHITE PAPER RUBRIC

	Expert	Competent	Emerging	Did not Meet Expectations	Score	Comments
Introduction/ Thesis	Exceptional introduction that grabs interest of reader and states topic. Thesis is exceptionally clear, arguable, well-developed, and a definitive statement.	Proficient introduction that is interesting and states topic. Thesis is clear and arguable statement of position.	Basic introduction that states topic but lacks interest. Thesis is somewhat clear and arguable.	Weak or no introduction of topic. Paper's purpose is unclear/thesis is weak or missing.		
Quality of Information/ Evidence	Paper is exceptionally researched, extremely detailed, and information provided is accurate. Information clearly relates to the thesis.	Information relates to the main topic. Paper is well-researched in detail and from a variety of sources.	Information relates to the main topic; few details and/or examples are given. Shows a limited variety of sources.	Information has little or nothing to do with the thesis. Information has weak or no connection to the thesis.		
Support of Thesis/Analysis	Exceptionally critical, relevant and consistent connections made between evidence and thesis. Excellent analysis.	Consistent connections made between evidence and thesis. Good analysis.	Some connections made between evidence and thesis. Some analysis.	Limited or no connections made between evidence and thesis. Lack of analysis.		
Organization/ Development of Thesis	Exceptionally clear, logical, mature, and thorough development of thesis with excellent transitions between and within paragraphs.	Clear and logical order that supports thesis with good transitions between and within paragraphs.	Somewhat clear and logical development with basic transitions between and within paragraphs.	Lacks development of ideas with weak or no transitions between and within paragraphs.		

Conclusion and Recommendations	Excellent summary of topic with sound and feasible recommendations that impact reader. Introduces no new information.	Good summary of topic with clear concluding ideas and recommendations. Introduces no new information.	Basic summary of topic with some final concluding ideas and one recommendation. Introduces no new information.	Lack of summary of topic. No recommendations.
Collaboration	Paper is clearly written with international partners as evidenced by inclusion of all partners' perspectives in data and recommendations.	Paper is written with international partners as evidenced by some inclusion of partners' perspectives in data and recommendations.	Limited evidence of collaboration between partners in the paper. Data presented and recommendations are largely from one perspective.	Little or no evidence of collaboration between partners in the paper. Data presented and recommendations are only from one perspective.
Grammar/Usage/ Mechanics	Control of grammar, usage, and mechanics. Almost entirely free of spelling, punctuation, and grammatical errors.	May contain few spelling, punctuation, and grammar errors.	Contains several spelling, punctuation, and grammar errors, which detract from the paper's readability.	So many spelling, punctuation, and grammar errors that the paper cannot be understood.

PRESENTATION RUBRIC

	Expert	Competent	Emerging	Did not Meet Expectations	Score	Comments
Evidence of Research Base	All content throughout the presentation is accurate. There are no factual errors. Clear evidence of research conducted and synthesized.	Most of the content is accurate but there is one piece of information that might be inaccurate. Evidence of research conducted, but limited synthesis is evident.	Content is generally accurate but there are several inconsistencies. Evidence of research conducted, but no synthesis is evident.	Little or no effort to present accurate content. Little evidence of research conducted, and no synthesis is evident.		
Content	Information is organized in a clear, logical way. It is easy to anticipate the type of material that might be on the next slide.	Most information is organized in a clear, logical way. One slide or item of information seems out of place.	Some information is logically sequenced. An occasional slide or item of information seems cut of place.	There is no clear plan for the organization of information.		

NATIONAL SCIENCE TEACHING ASSOCIATION

Presentation	Presentation flows smoothly. All presenters are involved relatively equally and presentation adheres to time frame.	Presentation flows smoothly. Presenters are involved relatively equally. Presentation is either over or under expected time frame.	Presentation is choppy at times. Presenters are not all involved substantively. Presentation is either over or under expected time frame.	Presentation is choppy throughout. Presenters are not all involved substantively. Presentation is greatly over or under expected time frame.
Recommendations	Excellent summary of topic with sound and feasible recommendations that impact reader. Introduces no new information.	Good summary of topic with clear concluding ideas and recommendations. Introduces no new information.	Basic summary of topic with some final concluding ideas and one recommendations. Introduces no new information.	Lack of summary of topic. No recommendations.
Collaboration	Presentation is clearly developed with international partners as evidenced by inclusion of all partners' perspectives in data and recommendations.	Presentation is developed with international partners as evidenced by some inclusion of partners' perspectives in data and recommendations.	Limited evidence of collaboration between partners in the presentation. Data presented and recommendations are largely from one perspective.	Little or no evidence of collaboration between partners in the presentation. Data presented and recommendations are only from one perspective.

REFERENCES

Conole, G., & Dyke, M. (2004). Understanding and using technological affordances: A response to Boyle and Cook. *ALT-J, Research in Learning Technology, 12*, 301–309. www.tandfonline.com/doi/full/10.1080/0968776042000216183

Peters-Burton, E. E., Seshaiyer, P., Burton, S. R., Drake-Patrick, J., & Johnson, C. C. (2015). The STEM road map for grades 9–12. In C. C. Johnson, E. E. Peters-Burton, & T. J. Moore (Eds.), *STEM road map: A framework for integrated STEM education* (pp. 124–162). Routledge.

TRANSFORMING LEARNING WITH CREATING GLOBAL BONDS AND THE *STEM ROAD MAP CURRICULUM SERIES*

Carla C. Johnson

This chapter serves as a conclusion to the Creating Global Bonds integrated STEM curriculum module, but it is just the beginning of the transformation of your classroom that is possible through use of the *STEM Road Map Curriculum Series.* In this book, many key resources have been provided to make learning meaningful for your students through integration of science, technology, engineering, and mathematics, as well as social studies and English language arts, into powerful problem- and project-based instruction. First, the Creating Global Bonds curriculum is grounded in the latest theory of learning for students in grade 12 specifically. Second, as your students work through this module, they engage in using the engineering design process (EDP) and build prototypes like engineers and STEM professionals in the real world. Third, students acquire important knowledge and skills grounded in national academic standards in mathematics, English language arts, science, and 21st century skills that will enable their learning to be deeper, retained longer, and applied throughout, illustrating the critical connections within and across disciplines. Finally, authentic formative assessments, including strategies for differentiation and addressing misconceptions, are embedded within the curriculum activities.

The Creating Global Bonds curriculum in the Sustainable Systems STEM Road Map theme can be used in single-content classrooms (e.g., mathematics) where there is only one teacher or expanded to include multiple teachers and content areas across classrooms. Through the exploration of the included lesson plans, students engage in a real-world STEM problem on the first day of instruction and gather necessary knowledge and skills along the way in the context of solving the problem.

DOI: 10.4324/9781003362371-9

The other topics in the *STEM Road Map Curriculum Series* are designed in a similar manner, and NSTA Press and Routledge have published additional volumes in this series for this and other grade levels, and have plans to publish more.

For an up-to-date list of volumes in the series, please visit www.routledge.com/STEM-Road-Map-Curriculum-Series/book-series/SRM (for titles co-published by Routledge and NSTA Press), or www.nsta.org/book-series/stem-road-map-curriculum (for titles published by NSTA Press).

If you are interested in professional development opportunities focused on the STEM Road Map specifically or integrated STEM or STEM programs and schools overall, contact the lead editor of this project, Dr. Carla C. Johnson, Professor of Science Education at NC State University. Someone from the team will be in touch to design a program that will meet your individual, school, or district needs.

INDEX

Page numbers in **bold** refer to tables.

For Product Safety Concerns and Information please contact our EU
representative GPSR@taylorandfrancis.com Taylor & Francis Verlag GmbH,
Kaufingerstraße 24, 80331 München, Germany

Batch number: 08159318

Printed by Printforce, the Netherlands